THE GOOD, THE BAD, AND THE UGLY
SAN FRANCISCO 49ERS

THE GOOD, THE BAD, AND THE UGLY
SAN FRANCISCO 49ERS

HEART-POUNDING, JAW-DROPPING, AND GUT-WRENCHING
MOMENTS FROM SAN FRANCISCO 49ERS HISTORY

Steven Travers
Foreword by Bob St. Clair

TRIUMPH
BOOKS

No part of this publication may be reproduced, stored in a retrieval system, or transmitted in any form by any means, electronic, mechanical, photocopying, or otherwise, without the prior written permission of the publisher, Triumph Books, 542 South Dearborn Street, Suite 750, Chicago, Illinois 60605.

Triumph Books and colophon are registered trademarks of Random House, Inc.

Library of Congress Cataloging-in-Publication Data

Travers, Steven.
  The good, the bad, and the ugly San Francisco 49ers: heart-pounding, jaw-dropping, and gut-wrenching moments from San Francisco 49ers history / Steven Travers ; foreword by Bob St. Clair.
     p. cm.
  ISBN 978-1-60078-279-4
  1. San Francisco 49ers (Football team)—History. 2. Football—California—San Francisco—History. I. Title.
  GV956.S3T73 2009
  796.332'640979461—dc22   2009028394

This book is available in quantity at special discounts for your group or organization. For further information, contact:

Triumph Books
542 South Dearborn Street, Suite 750
Chicago, Illinois 60605
(312) 939–3330 | Fax (312) 663–3557
www.triumphbooks.com

Printed in U.S.A.
ISBN: 978-1-60078-279-4
Design by Patricia Frey
Editorial production by Prologue Publishing Services, LLC
All photos courtesy of Getty Images unless otherwise noted

To my good friend Mike McDowd
A true 49ers faithful

CONTENTS

FOREWORD

In the spring of 1953 I received a call from Pete Rozelle, who at the time was the public-relations director for the Los Angeles Rams. He told me that the Rams were looking at me and to hang tight. As it turned out, L.A. selected a 6'4", 235-pound offensive tackle out of Kentucky (in the third round) by the name of Bob Fry.

Before the Rams could select again, I had already been drafted by the 49ers and would be returning to my hometown of San Francisco. Owner Tony Morabito offered me $5,500. I told him no. I wanted $6,000 because a former teammate of mine at Tulsa, Marv Matuszak, signed with Pittsburgh for that amount. Mr. Morabito hung up the phone. A week later he called back and agreed to the $6,000-per-year contract. I just may have been the league's first holdout!

When I reported to the 49ers as a rookie in 1953, I immediately was matched one-on-one against Leo Nomellini. Leo was an All-Pro tackle. He weighed 265 pounds and was counted on to give me my initiation into the NFL.

One of the major problems that we faced in those days was that we only had 33 players on a team. This meant playing both offense, defense, and all special teams.

In my first three years I not only played both offense and defense but rarely left the field throughout the entire four quarters. And as far as playing on special teams, that was an automatic. There wasn't really any room for a guy who could only play one position. The "specialist" had not yet come of age.

The game back then was built around roughness. I used to leg-whip in those days—and it was legal! But I was handicapped by the way I had to block. Offensive linemen couldn't use their hands. I would have loved to have played the way they do today. There was also a personal high about knocking a man down—really hitting him hard. It was the only satisfaction an offensive lineman had. It gave you a jolt of the ol' adrenaline.

I consider myself very fortunate to have played in the 1950s and to have been a part of a team with some of the greatest football players of all time. Our quarterback was Y.A. Tittle, our halfback was Hugh "the King" McElhenny, and our fullbacks were Joe "the Jet" Perry and John Henry Johnson. They were known as the "Million Dollar Backfield," and they are the only complete backfield enshrined in the Pro Football Hall of Fame.

I also had the opportunity to play with some of the other 49ers legends—R.C. Owens, the receiving half of the alley-oop pass; Billy Wilson, a Hall of Fame–caliber end; and defensive back Jimmy Johnson and defensive lineman Leo Nomellini, both in the Hall of Fame. There were others—John David Crow, Ed Henke, Dicky Moegle, Ted Connolly, Bruce Bosley, Gordy Soltau, Abe Woodson, Joe Arenas, Clay Matthews, Charlie Krueger, John Brodie, J.D. Smith, Eddie Dove, Billy Kilmer, Don Burke, Roland Lakes, Bob Toneff, Clyde Connor, Visco Grgich, and Bruno Banducci (now there's a name that goes way back)—just to name a few.

I was a member of the 49ers from 1953 to 1964, and I wouldn't change playing in my era for any other. But every so often I get questions from people wondering how my era would have fared compared to today's. Well, let's look at it this way: I played both offense and defense predominately the whole game. We didn't have face masks the first three years, our helmets were leather, and we had numerous injuries we had to play through. Now, I don't think the question should be whether or not we could play in today's league. I think the question should be whether or not these "candy asses" of today could play with us!

—Bob St. Clair
Pro Football Hall of Fame, 1990

ACKNOWLEDGMENTS

Thanks to Tom Bast, Don Gulbrandsen, and all the great folks at Triumph Books and Random House Publishing for having faith in me. Thank you to Jennifer Barrell at Prologue Publishing Services. I want to thank the San Francisco 49ers, a class organization. Thanks to John and Jean Strahlendorf and the 49ers Booster Clubs. Thanks to Ken Flower. Thanks to Hall of Famer Bob St. Clair and Dr. Kristine Setting Clark.

Thanks to Karen Peterson for website support.

Of course, my thanks as always go out to my daughter, Elizabeth Travers; my parents, Don and Inge Travers; and to my Lord and Savior, Jesus Christ, who has shed his grace on thee, and to whom all glory is due!

INTRODUCTION: HIPPIES, A PARK, AND A FOOTBALL TEAM

t starts with my dad, a native San Franciscan. As a young man, he ushered 49ers games at Kezar Stadium. The Rams, the Eagles, the Packers...he saw them all. Pro football on the West Coast. For my old man, a Cal grad who played alongside Sam Chapman and Vic Bottari—and who rooted for Pappy Waldorf's teams, for Johnny Olszewski—well, this was something new. Bob Waterfield versus Frankie Albert. Joe Perry. Bruno Banducci.

Donald E. Travers became a successful track and cross-country coach at Lowell and then at Balboa High School in the City, then taught at CCSF. Bob Troppmann, who later was Pete Carroll's coach at Redwood High, did his student teaching under my dad. Dad was part of a golden age—helping an injured prep runner named Johnny Mathis off the Kezar track, a USF superstar named Ollie Matson, a junior-college flame named O.J. Simpson.

My dad's father, Charles Stevens Travers, had once covered the 1906 Great Earthquake for the *San Francisco Call* before becoming president of the San Francisco Press Club. He was in his eighties when I knew him, living on Parnassus Avenue next to UC–San Francisco Medical School. Every Sunday my mom drove me to see him. We would drive through Golden Gate Park, past gyrating hippies who were tripping on LSD and pot. My mother would try to shield my eyes from the sight of naked girls dancing in the hazy sunshine, with Kezar as a backdrop. It was the Summer of Love.

During the football season, I could see the Niners games on the green plains of Kezar from Grandaddy's balcony. The whole football experience for a kid growing up in San Francisco was different than that of a kid in Green Bay or South Bend or Chicago, that's for sure. My Christmas present from my dad in 1970 was two tickets to the NFC Championship Game at Kezar between the 49ers and Cowboys. Dallas' "Doomsday Defense" was impenetrable, and Craig Morton was just effective enough, along with Duane Thomas, to give Dallas a 17–10 win. The Kezar crowd was rude, drunk, and violent—fighting, bottles thrown through the air, foul language. It was very family-unfriendly, at least as much so as the current Raider Nation. Fans were openly yelling for the Niners to "hurt Morton." It was ugly and an eye-opener for a kid.

A few years later, I attended the University of Southern California. In 1978 my dad came to L.A. for Thanksgiving weekend. We watched the Trojans play Notre Dame for the national championship. For three quarters USC and Ronnie Lott dominated the Irish. Then Joe Montana brought them back all the way. The only other college performance I have ever personally seen that compares was Vince Young's 2006 Rose Bowl against USC.

Driving back to Santa Monica in the gloaming, I told my father that I did not care where Montana was drafted, that he was a future NFL hero. No question, Montana possessed undeniable magic, charisma, and star quality. I knew enough about sports to know it when I saw it. It was like seeing Marlon Brando for the first time, or Ronald Reagan making "the Speech" in 1964.

'SC managed to win that day on the strength of a field goal by a history major from San Francisco's Riordan High School named Frank Jordan. To this day, Jordan's winning kick is enshrined on the wall of Harding Park's golf clubhouse. It must have been a moment of conundrum in the Irish Sunset District!

Back to Montana. He was *the good*. Joe, of course, was more than good. He was, for my money, the very best quarterback in pro football history. I am no provincial type; I know the arguments on behalf of Baugh, Graham, Unitas...Staubach and Bradshaw...Elway and Marino. I'll take Joe. I think you will, too.

THE GOOD

THE CATCH

When it comes to the San Francisco 49ers, everything comes down to this day, this game, this moment: the Catch. It is the Holy Grail of the franchise, the parting of the Red Sea by which a flood of glory days follow.

The date was January 10, 1982. It had been an unusually rainy season in the Bay Area. Major floods created havoc on the Russian River and in Marin County just two weeks earlier, but the City was drying out when the Dallas Cowboys rode into town for the NFC Championship Game.

The Cowboys were still the Cowboys. Roger Staubach was no longer their quarterback, replaced by Danny White, but Tom Landry was their coach, and they had all the swagger of the 1970s teams that went to five Super Bowls and won two of them.

Up until that day, the 49ers were suspect. They had been desultory in the mid- to late 1970s. Bill Walsh was a successful college coach, but by no means the Genius. They were coming off a 6–10 year and under Joe Montana had gone 13–3, but Joe was not yet the Greatest Quarterback of All Time.

This was Caesar crossing the Rubicon, Grant taking Richmond, the von Rundstedt Plan in 1914. It was San Francisco's bid for immortality.

While the 49ers are remembered for the offensive exploits of Montana, it was defense that powered them. Jerry Rice was years from becoming a Niner. They had little in the way of a running game. But they had a rookie defensive back from USC named Ronnie Lott, who put the fear of God in opposing ball carriers. Veterans Fred Dean and Jack "Hacksaw" Reynolds had come over via trades. Hungry for championships that had eluded them throughout their careers, they spurred the team on.

"Going to the 49ers was like a breath of fresh air for me, a new start," said Dean. "They were underestimated in '81, and we took a lot of teams by surprise. But by the Dallas game, people knew we were for real. That game was important to the franchise. And the Catch? Well, the Catch was the most important play of the season. Getting to the Super Bowl is every player's dream. It was the Catch that put us there."

The Catch was thrown by Joe Montana, whose name resonates in the world of sports and celebrity like that of Babe Ruth, Joe DiMaggio, Muhammad Ali, and Michael Jordan. But the Catch was made by Dwight Clark. Clark was a Southerner out of Clemson University. Nineteen eighty-one was a particularly good year for him, as his pro team, San Francisco, went all the way the same year his alma mater captured an equally improbable national title.

Clark is an all-time great 49er who went on to a successful front-office career, but unlike Montana, he lives off the Catch

HALL OF THE VERY GOOD

Dwight Clark was a 6'4", 204-pound receiver drafted 10th in the 1979 draft by the 49ers out of Clemson University. Clark obviously is a 49ers legend because he made the Catch against Dallas in the January 1982 NFC Championship Game. Clark played for San Francisco until 1987 and was Joe Montana's best friend. Later, he was a high-ranking, well-respected 49ers executive, a protégé of Bill Walsh. But Clark was not a Hall of Famer, as in a Canton Hall of Famer. He was not particularly fast, and while talented, he was a product of Walsh's system. When Jerry Rice and John Taylor came along, Montana had better targets. As good as the team was with Dwight, they were better with Rice and Taylor.

above all other accomplishments. He is like Bobby Thomson and his "Shot Heard 'Round the World," or the Craig Fertig–Rod Sherman combination who teamed up to throw and catch the winning touchdown for Southern California, ending Notre Dame's title hopes in 1964.

Clark remembered feeling "very confident," and felt his team matured that day in ways that resonated not just in the subsequent Super Bowl win over Cincinnati, but in the entire Team-of-the-Decade 1980s.

The 49ers had struggled early in the season, although those September struggles were successes compared to the dismal previous eight years. They lost to Cleveland at home in November, prompting a rendition of hometown band Journey's "Don't Stop Believing," as fans filed out of Candlestick. But by that time, they won a defensive struggle at Green Bay and beat the Steelers.

The turning-point win at Pittsburgh, according to Clark, was the game that propelled them to ultimate victory. Pittsburgh was the Team of the 1970s.

Now they were facing America's Team, Dallas.

"I could never describe in words what it was like," Clark recalled. "At the time, it happened so fast, it's hard to put into words. On the other hand, I look back, and everything happens in slow motion. My friends always kid me that the play could have been 'the Drop.'"

Football fans watching on national television got a good look at the contrast in climate between the Midwest and the Pacific Coast. The early AFC title game featured the warm-weather San Diego Chargers almost freezing to death in their loss at Cincinnati to a Bengals team that probably would not have beaten Dan Fouts & Co. on a neutral field. After that "ice bowl," the relatively sunsplashed Candlestick looked like paradise. It at least offered even playing conditions.

San Francisco started things in good form when Montana hit Freddie Solomon for an eight-yard touchdown pass 4:19 into the first quarter. Dallas clawed back in with a field goal. A 49ers fumble set up a two-play drive. Ex–Arizona State quarterback White hit Tony Hill from the 26: 10–7, Dallas.

San Francisco sputtered as the two teams settled into trench warfare, but the Niners' historian-coach, Bill Walsh, knew he needed a football version of the Meuse-Argonne Offensive in order to give his team confidence that they could beat Tom Landry's Cowboys. Unable to move the ball on the ground, and with the vaunted West Coast offense out of sync, he called for a big play and got it: Montana bootlegging to the right, finding Clark deep for 38 yards. But Dallas met the challenge and held. Sixty thousand fans groaned, and "it could be heard for miles down the Bayshore Freeway from the Stick," wrote Michael Tuckman and Jeff Schultz in *The San Francisco 49ers: Team of the Decade.*

"That was a little depressing," said linebacker Keena Turner.

Back to the trenches. On Dallas' next possession, San Francisco won the battle. With field position shifting in their favor, Montana knew he needed to take advantage of it. Starting at the Dallas 47, he put it all together in the style that he would come to be known for. Montana could overcome confusion, replacing it with vision, like no other. The result this time was a four-play touchdown drive, with Joe scrambling out of the pocket to his left, mostly avoiding Everson Walls (whose interception interrupted the last drive). With Dallas committed to the rush, Clark was wide open if only Montana could unload it, which he did, but not without paying the price in the form of some 1,000 pounds of blue-and-white Dallas beef on top of him. When the crowd went wild, Montana—under the pile—knew he had succeeded, and perhaps those Cowboy pass rushers knew that the man buried beneath them was truly special.

"I kinda like when that happens," Montana said.

America's Team had no intention of relinquishing the throne easily. After an 80-yard drive, their own Hall of Famer, running back Tony Dorsett, scored from the 5, and they led again, 17–14.

Ronnie Lott made a rare mistake when he was flagged for pass interference to help Dallas keep the drive alive. Later, Lott questioned the call, as did Walsh. Walsh saw that the game would be won not by the infantry but by the air force. After the half, he had tried for a big strike, but Montana was intercepted. So was White.

Wide receiver Dwight Clark may be best known for one play—"The Catch" that beat the Cowboys in the 1981 NFC Championship—but he had a stellar nine-year NFL career, all with the 49ers. His final numbers: 506 receptions, 6,750 yards, and 48 touchdowns.

It was not a perfectly played game, but the adrenaline was at a fever pitch with the realization that the struggle would go on to the end.

San Francisco struck with a two-yard Johnny Davis touchdown run to lead 21–17, but nobody felt safe.

"Going back and forth like that with the score, it must have been fun to watch," said Turner. Maybe for fans of the Bears, or perhaps Bengals supporters already secure in their team's Super Bowl fortunes.

A slight 49ers edge was gained when Dallas was held to a Rafael Septien field goal, cutting it to a razor-thin 21–20. When San Francisco fumbled in the fourth quarter and Dallas converted it into a 21-yard touchdown pass from White to tight end Doug Cosbie, the game had all the earmarks of past 49ers horrors: blowing the 1957 NFL playoff game to Detroit; letting Roger Staubach destroy them in 1972. Their opponents were the masters of the fourth-quarter comeback, the two-minute drill, the thrill-a-minute comeback.

But this time, the 49ers had Joe.

"They took the lead, and a big hush came over the crowd, and it was as if the coffin had closed on our season," tight end Charle "Tree" Young, now a preacher who speaks in a dramatic pulpit manner. With Montana, however, "We rose to the occasion. Nothing could stop us."

What is often forgotten, however, is that Montana did not lead San Francisco to victory right after Cosbie's catch. He threw a seeming game-breaking interception. Landry decided that *their* infantry would close it out. For nine excruciating plays, Dallas held the ball, the lead, and time of possession. There was no room for error; a Septien field goal

TOP 10 NORTHERN CALIFORNIA SPORTS OWNERS

1. Al Davis, Oakland Raiders
2. Charlie O. Finley, Oakland A's
3. Edward DeBartolo Jr., San Francisco 49ers
4. Peter Magowan, San Francisco Giants
5. Walter Haas, Oakland A's
6. Franklin Mieuli, San Francisco/Golden State Warriors
7. Horace Stoneham, San Francisco Giants
8. Lou Spadia, San Francisco 49ers
9. Joe & Gavin Maloof, Sacramento Kings
10. Lew Wolff, Oakland A's

would ice it. The big crowd expected the worst. After all, this was San Francisco, not across-the-bay Oakland where the comeback win was as commonplace as it was in Dallas.

But San Francisco held. Solomon fair caught Danny White's punt at the 49ers' 11 with 4:54 to go. The lights were on in the January gloaming; a crowd begged, a nation waited to see the presence of greatness. Montana had shown more than glimpses of it on national TV before: in 1977 when he led Notre Dame to the national championship; in 1978 in a noble defeat against USC; in 1979 against Houston in a college performance perhaps unrivaled in history.

Walsh kept it short. The West Coast offense churned up yards—and time—to midfield. With two minutes left, they were in Cowboys territory. Dallas, like the Romans more than 2,000 years earlier, were determined to keep the modern version of Hannibal in the Italian countryside. Montana was determined to be the Carthaginian who broke through the gates. The duel was personal on the sideline; the defensive mastermind Landry versus the new passing guru of the West, Walsh.

Solomon gained 14 on a reverse, Clark caught a 10-yarder, and then Solomon caught a 12-yarder to the Dallas 13. A timeout was called with 1:15 to play. The field was now narrowed to the defensive advantage.

Montana threw an incomplete pass, but Lenvil Elliott gained seven on a sweep to the 6. Another timeout was called. Faced with defeat or glory, the two legends-to-be, Montana and Walsh, decided to go for Solomon in the air. Walsh told Montana to hold on to the ball until the last possible instant, looking for the speedy Solomon, but if he was covered, the secondary receiver should be Clark. If the Clark option was exercised, however, "hold it or throw it high" so that "it'll be thrown away" instead of intercepted, with another play to go to if this failed, according to Walsh.

According to offensive tackle Keith Fahnhorst, the huddle was bristling with confidence, which no doubt can be attributed to Montana and also to Walsh. "Sprint right motion" was set up for Clark to line up slot on the right, run an inside hook, with

WINNERS

Edward J. DeBartolo Jr. was a flawed human being, but nobody can argue that he was one of the most effective owners of a sports franchise in the history of Northern California. He came from Youngstown, Ohio, a town notorious for organized crime. DeBartolo's family made their millions through real estate, mostly shopping centers. The term "mob ties" has attached itself to his name, possibly unfairly because he is Italian. He liked to party, was known to favor strippers, and got in some trouble from time to time, but the players loved him. He paid them well, beginning with his 1977 purchase of the club and on through their Team-of-the-Decade, four–Super Bowl, 1980s dominance.

Solomon taking three steps and then heading up the sideline. Walsh wanted something that would be deep in the end zone for either man. Landry gambled that his rushers would get to Joe before he could find Solomon or Clark. With almost any other quarterback, he would have been right.

Ed "Too Tall" Jones, however, "looped" around the linebackers, recalled Fahnhorst, but when Earl Cooper blocked his man, he also knocked Fahnhorst down. Solomon slipped, and Clark was double-covered. Montana sprinted to the right, chased by Dallas defenders like giant policemen hoping to bring down a robber. D.D. Lewis was a few feet from Montana. The sideline approached dangerously, looking like the ground approaching a skydiver whose parachute was not yet open. Montana kept his cool. He had an extra play if he had to go out of bounds or throw it away, but he did not want to waste the play unless he had to. If he went out of bounds or was sacked, the loss of yards would be an obstacle almost impossible to overcome. Instead of giving up, Montana then backpedaled a few feet. Solomon was covered, but Clark broke free.

Montana unloaded one for the 6'4" Clark, tossing it high enough to avoid an interception but seemingly beyond Dwight's reach. Montana later said he was surprised that Clark had to "jump that high," disputing the notion that it was a throwaway, and thus a fluke.

Montana, sitting under some 520 pounds of high-priced Dallas defense, did not see it, but observed replays, marveling at Clark's leaping ability. As great as Montana was, it is called "the Catch," not "the Pass," because it was Clark's superlative leap and sure hands that brought it down.

"I thought I had jumped too soon," recalled Clark, but he came down with it.

The Stick went utterly ballistic. All-Pro center Randy Cross had been knocked on his keister and was a spectator.

"I saw the whole thing," said Cross. "It was really pretty."

The extra point gave San Francisco a 28–27 lead, but the collective conscience of millions pictured Dallas making a patented Cowboy comeback to win on a field goal by the reliable Septien. When the kick was returned to midfield, it looked somewhere between possible and probable, but White was not Staubach, and San Francisco held.

Rookies Lott, Eric Wright, Carlton Williamson, Lynn Thomas, and second-year man Montana represented an incredible future. Clark was now an instant legend.

"That one play didn't make me financially wealthy or anything," said Clark when his No. 87 was retired on "Dwight Clark Day" at Candlestick in 1988. "I didn't all of a sudden get a ton of commercials. But not a single person who knows anything about football doesn't know about the Catch."

BIRTH OF A DYNASTY

The San Francisco 49ers' victory over the Cincinnati Bengals at the Pontiac Silverdome in Michigan on January 24, 1982, at first appeared to be just another surprise world championship by a previously bad sports team. Obviously Bill Walsh was the "flavor of the day" among coaches, Joe Montana was an emerging star, and Ronnie Lott had the makings of greatness; but overall there was scant evidence that a dynasty was in the works. They had little running game and did not have the star power of the great teams of the 1970s: the Steelers, Cowboys, Raiders, and Dolphins.

But as it turned out, San Francisco's victory served as harbinger of more than simply the franchise's ascendancy. It was a paradigm shift in Bay Area sensibilities. Up until 1982, virtually all sports greatness in Northern California resided in Oakland. The Giants had made their bid in 1962, falling just short, but in the 1970s they were a joke, playing in dilapidated Candlestick while their rivals, the Dodgers, rose to a position of glamour; winning pennants in front of capacity crowds and an admiring Hollywood crowd at beautiful Dodger Stadium.

Oakland billed itself as the "Home of Champions" for good reason. The A's captured three straight world championships (1972, 1973, and 1974), the Warriors one NBA title (1975), and the Raiders two Super Bowl victories (1976 and 1980). San Francisco had lost the Warriors to the East Bay in the early 1970s. The Rams dominated San Francisco and played a "hometown" Super Bowl at the Rose Bowl in 1980. USC and UCLA just killed California and Stanford. Los Angeles was seen as the most trend-setting American city, surpassing crime-infested New York with no competition from San Francisco. In 1982 they "stole" the Raiders.

The City was at a low point. Political power resided in the Southland, where Los Angelenos Richard Nixon and Ronald Reagan had ascended to the White House. San Francisco's national image was one of corruption and ineptitude, its streets dirty and filled with the homeless. In 1977 Superintendent Harvey Milk and Mayor George Moscone were shot to death by a colleague who avoided a murder conviction using the "Twinkie defense," but later committed suicide. Clint Eastwood's *Dirty Harry* series did little for the City's image. San Francisco's Financial District lacked the panache of Wall Street. Its restaurants and nightspots were "so yesterday." Tourists and suburbanites found little appeal. Strip clubs were controlled by organized crime. Broadway was dangerous. Polk Street was a haven for "anything goes."

DID YOU KNOW...

That the 1981 49ers featured three rookies in the secondary? Aside from Ronnie Lott, there was Carlton Williamson and Eric Wright.

San Francisco Bay Area sports fans resorted to class envy and boorishness. Cal students dumbly waved credit cards in an effort

BUSINESS COMES FIRST

The 49ers got off to a hopeful start in 1981, but nobody knew if they were for real. Then they traded a 1983 No. 2 draft pick and option to exchange 1983 No. 1 draft choices to the San Diego Chargers for veteran defensive end Fred Dean. All Dean did was earn the UPI Defensive Player of the Year award, the NFL Outstanding Defensive Lineman of the Year award, the NFC Defensive Player of the Year award, and a Pro Bowl spot. Another key acquisition was linebacker Jack "Hacksaw" Reynolds, a longtime Rams nemesis. He and Dean anchored the defense with Lott in the secondary.

to "mock" the rich USC kids, who just laughed at them. Giants fans showed up for the Dodgers and little else. They threw garbage at Tommy Lasorda, soiling the air with foul epithets, impressing nobody who counted.

When the San Francisco 49ers won the 1982 Super Bowl, however, it all started to change. Thousands of people descended on the City. Cars jammed the Broadway tunnel, and people celebrated at the Triangle in the manner of patriots on V-J Day. It was this event that created the birth, or renaissance, of the trendy, yuppie Marina District, Cow Hollow, and Pacific Heights areas. In conjunction with the computer revolution, it led to the gentrification of Broadway, the growth south of Market, and eventually the building of Pacific Bell Park in 2000.

It is not inconceivable to state that the popularity of the Montana-Walsh-Lott 49ers created conditions leading to political revitalization, spurring city growth and leading to the City's hosting of the 1984 Democratic National Convention and two San Francisco women, Dianne Feinstein and Barbara Boxer, being elected to the U.S. Senate. Los Angeles lost clout amid riots, a major earthquake, the O.J. murders, dry spells at USC and UCLA, and the loss of both the Rams and Raiders.

It had started a few years earlier when Eddie DeBartolo, scion of a shopping center empire in a town notorious for organized crime—Youngstown, Ohio—improbably spent $16 million to take

The San Francisco defense celebrates a third-quarter goal-line stand that kept Cincinnati out of the end zone and helped seal the 49ers' first Super Bowl victory, a 26–21 decision over the Bengals on January 25, 1982. Photo courtesy of AP Images.

over the Niners. The "carpetbagging" DeBartolo had hit all the right buttons, however. Bill Walsh came over from Stanford. Joe Montana was still available when Walsh took him in the third round. Walsh scooped Ronnie Lott up in the draft like a hungry man presented a free cheeseburger and fries at Original Joe's. Seattle took UCLA's Kenny Easley, who they felt was a better prospect.

In 1981 everything clicked: 13–3 to win the West; slaying the Rams; victory over Dallas; and a trip to Michigan, where the NFL had gambled that a Super Bowl party could be pulled off despite frozen conditions. Had the game been played outdoors, Cincinnati may well have prevailed as they had against San Diego at Riverfront Stadium, but the Silverdome was just that...a dome.

"It was definitely a new experience for us," said Keena Turner. Walsh broke the tension by meeting his team at the hotel dressed as a bellhop. His calming influence kept the team focused even when a traffic jam through the snow-covered streets caused San Francisco to arrive at the Silverdome late.

The Bengals were not from a major media market, and San Francisco's sports enthusiasm was questioned, but surprisingly the ratings were high to see the New Order after years of Steelers, Cowboys, Raiders, and Dolphins domination. Fans were interested in Walsh and Montana. Walsh scripted the first 20 plays or so, and it worked to perfection. San Francisco sprinted out to a 20–0 halftime lead, threatening to turn the game into a rout.

"We felt satisfied that we'd done what we wanted to do in the first half," recalled Fred Dean.

Hacksaw Reynolds, however, had played on a Rams squad that had gotten off to a good start before losing to Pittsburgh in the Pasadena Super Bowl two years earlier. He knew the game was not over.

Cincinnati got the ball to start the second half. Led by quarterback Ken Anderson, they drove 83 yards to make the score 20–7. For a young team, panic was a natural component, the threat of blowing a big lead hanging over their heads.

Cincinnati seemed to have solved Montana: Ross Browner sacked him, and a pass to Freddie Solomon was broken up.

"We definitely lost our momentum at that point," said Turner.

Another three-and-out and field position advantage to Cincinnati made DeBartolo suddenly stop thinking of victory speeches. Anderson went after the 49ers' young secondary, hitting receiver Cris Collinsworth for 49 yards to the 49ers' 14. Cincinnati worked their way down to the 3, first-and-goal.

Big Pete Johnson, perhaps the best power runner in the NFL in such a situation, was sent up the middle. He had scored more touchdowns at Ohio State than Archie Griffin. He pulled a coterie of 49ers with him to the 1.

"Everybody was pretty hyped up in the huddle," said Dean. "My feeling was, either we could stop them here and be champs, or we could lose it and think about it for the rest of our lives."

Ex-Packer and now Bengals coach Forrest Gregg no doubt wanted a repeat of Bart Starr's quarterback sneak for a touchdown that overcame Dallas' goal-line stand in the 1967 Ice Bowl. After Johnson's carry, Gregg decided that he would play it as a four-down situation—touchdown or nothing. Johnson got the ball behind left guard Dave Lapham, but John Harty, Dwaine Board, and Archie Reese met him. Harty brought him down, no gain.

Former LSU star Charles Alexander "the Great" got the ball on a swing pass and ran wide. Linebacker Dan Bunz, a blond kid who looked like a typical Southern California beach boy from unheralded Long Beach State, had lost his starting job. This would be his only tackle of the game. He would not be an All-Pro, Canton was not waiting, greatness was not his destiny, but in the annals of 49ers lore, his stop of Alexander in the open field ranks with the Catch or any of Montana's touchdown tosses.

Alexander had blundered by cutting off his pattern before he could reach paydirt. Now it was fourth-and-goal. Momentum favored San Francisco, but Pete Johnson was a momentum-buster. He hit the line hard, but it was crowded, and he was stopped by Hacksaw Reynolds. Archie Reese rolled onto the pile, waving his arms in exultation.

The 49ers' sideline went nuts.

"We were ecstatic!" exclaimed Randy Cross.

"From that point on, we realized we could win this thing," said wide receiver Mike Shumann.

The inches differential reminds one of Al Pacino's locker room speech to his team in *Any Given Sunday*, a film coproduced by ex-49er Jamie Williams.

"You've gotta fight for those inches," Pacino's Tony D'Amato says. "Because those inches are the difference between winnin' and losin'...between livin' and dyin'."

So true.

The poor field position left San Francisco vulnerable when they were unable to move the ball, allowing Cincinnati to come back and score to make it 20–14. But the goal-line stand had given them confidence. The kickoff field position was restored, allowing two modest 49ers drives that were just enough to allow Ray

WINNERS

Charle "Tree" Young was a prototype tight end who came out of Edison High School in Fresno to the University of Southern California, where he played in the famed 1970 game at Alabama that is credited with ending segregation in southern football. He was an All-American in 1972—"I only got two or three passes a game, but averaged 20 yards a reception," he said. The '72 Trojans are considered the greatest team in college football history. Charle played for the Philadelphia Eagles and the Los Angeles Rams. He participated in the 1980 Super Bowl for the Rams before coming over to San Francisco. A total team player, he was used mainly as a blocker but was a key element in Bill Walsh's West Coast offense and a member of the 1981 world champions. He finished his career in Seattle, where he is to this day a respected Christian minister.

Wersching to kick two field goals and put the game out of reach for Cincinnati.

Cincinnati scored late to close it to 26–21, but Walsh's team hung on for the first world championship in city history. The only other "ultimate championship" won by a team within San Francisco city limits was USF's 1955–1956 NCAA basketball titles, led by Bill Russell and K.C. Jones.

Not only had the 49ers shed their losers' image, they had shed San Francisco's loser's image; or more appropriately, restored its image as a great city, tarnished in recent years. Suddenly, the Genius, Bill Walsh, and the golden boy from Notre Dame, Joe Montana, represented S.F. excellence in the manner of local boys like Joe DiMaggio and Frank Crosetti...names seemingly from a bygone era that was no more, at least until the Niners brought glory back to the City by the Bay.

As if carried by the new popularity of San Francisco, local acts such as Huey Lewis and the News and Journey seemed to be propelled to national stardom on the backs of the 49ers. A new golden era had begun. The people who descended on the City's streets and bars the night of January 24, 1982, felt a new energy that would indeed lift the entire region over the next 15 years.

THE GREATEST QUARTERBACK WHO EVER LIVED

By and large, when modern pundits ponder the question or create Internet polls to determine who the greatest quarterback who ever lived might be, the name most often mentioned is Joe Montana.

This in and of itself does not mean that Joe is indeed the greatest signal-caller ever. It is a subjective barroom argument; fun to talk about, not something that can be conclusively "proved" like the nature of gravity, or the density of atoms, or the like.

Nevertheless, when one factors everything into the equation, it becomes apparent that Montana may well be the most logical choice for this most lofty perch in the football hierarchy.

In order for a sports historian to state that Joe is the best, the historian must possess good knowledge of those who came before and after him. Otherwise, to say Joe is the best is just an empty comment.

"Slingin' Sammy" Baugh certainly has his supporters. He changed the nature of the game from ground-oriented to an aerial show. His style was flamboyant and versatile. Quarterbacks like Sid Luckman and Bob Waterfield were fabulous practitioners of the football arts. Many have argued the greatness of Cleveland's Otto Graham, a consummate team leader and field general who controlled the flow of his team's offense in masterful style.

The great Johnny Unitas of Baltimore probably holds up as Montana's toughest "competition." Johnny U. combined great statistics with winning ways (his teams won championships) and the ability to direct the Colts to victory in the late minutes of come-from-behind contests.

In the 1960s, with the advent of the American Football League, a series of talented longball artists dominated the pro scene, among them Daryle Lamonica of Oakland, Joe Namath of the New York Jets, Len Dawson of Kansas City, Bart Starr of Green Bay, and Sonny Jurgensen of Washington.

More all-time greats emerged in the 1970s: Terry Bradshaw of Pittsburgh, Bob Griese of Miami, Ken Stabler of Oakland, Roger Staubach of Dallas, and Fran Tarkenton of Minnesota.

Then came Joe. He too played in an era in which other great quarterbacks competed against him. Miami's Dan Marino and Denver's John Elway could not beat Montana, but their lifetime statistics were gaudier. Joe Theismann came along and had his moments. Several other quarterbacks led teams to Super Bowl victories in the 1980s and 1990s but were unable to sustain greatness over a period of years.

With the retirements of Montana, Marino, Elway, and San Francisco's Steve Young, it does not appear that the new breed of NFL quarterback is as good as those who came before. Several mobile, athletic quarterbacks have appeared in recent years. Michael Vick of Atlanta seemed to be headed for greatness until he met trouble the way the *Titanic* met an iceberg. Donovan McNabb of Philadelphia changed the parameters of the position in accordance with new realities; namely, that defensive backs are now so fast that modern QBs either must reduce the steps they drop back into the pocket or be fast enough to make plays once flushed out of it.

More traditional pocket passers like Ben Roethlisberger of Pittsburgh, or New England's Tom Brady (at least until his 2008 injury) have been favorably compared to Montana; their legacies promise to be good ones, but there appears no "replacements" for Montana in the offing.

It always seems to come back to Joe. He was an artist, a da Vinci. He had undeniable magic: on-field charisma. He was not the biggest, nor the fastest; by no means did he possess the strongest arm. Montana himself, as well as his coaches and teammates, will say that much of his greatness stemmed from his surroundings: great teammates; just the right coach; a system designed for him; a perfect storm of time, place, and events that produced the most effective winning machine in football history.

After all, this is what it all comes down to: winning. The San Francisco 49ers of the 1980s were probably the finest single-decade team in history. Cleveland dominated the 1950s, Green Bay the 1960s, Pittsburgh the 1970s, and New England has made a bid in the 2000s, but none did it quite the way the 49ers did it in the 1980s.

Montana carried the winning tradition into the 1990s, a decade not dominated by any single team. But the 49ers picked right up where Bill Walsh and Montana left off—their 1994 Super Bowl championship team and others who competed at a similar level—right up until the later years of the decade. In many ways the legacy of his rival and successor, Steve Young, is a reflection of Montana. Fairly or unfairly, Graham, Unitas, Starr, Staubach, Bradshaw, Marino, and Elway—the quarterbacks who must be regarded as Montana's competition for the "all-time greatest" label, never had a successor to rival what Young did. In some ways they are like presidents who are not succeeded by a member of their party. Montana's legacy, on the other hand, was upheld by Young.

Montana was a winner. He made the 49ers winners. His influence was so great that they won when he left.

"My father wasn't always telling me to win, win, win—he wasn't force-feeding me," he said. "It was more of a teaching process, and the lesson was to strive to win: to know that the only way to accomplish anything in sports is to be a winner. If a quarterback sets all kinds of individual records but plays for a losing team, the public and the media—in all their infinite wisdom—are likely to brand the guy a loser. Nobody had ever had the kind of season Dan Marino did before the Dolphins played us in the '85 Super Bowl. But he had a lousy Super Bowl. We won, and people began to doubt him.

RETIRED 49ERS JERSEYS

8	Steve Young
12	John Brodie
16	Joe Montana
34	Joe Perry
37	Jimmy Johnson
39	Hugh McElhenny
42	Ronnie Lott
70	Charlie Krueger
73	Leo Nomellini
79	Bob St. Clair
87	Dwight Clark

Another example is Fran Tarkenton, a great player and a successful businessman. He brought a new dimension to the quarterback position. But when people talk about his playing days, they'll always wind up saying, somewhere in the conversation, that he never won a Super Bowl with the Vikings."

Montana reiterated that the only thing separating "chumps from champions" are those who love to compete and, in the end, win. Whether luck or something else had anything to do with it, Montana won four Super Bowls. Marino ended up like Tarkenton, a man who set many of the records Marino broke, but like Fran, he never won the ultimate game.

Montana "may be the greatest player who ever the played the game," said broadcaster and former Bengals receiver Cris Collinsworth.

"Joe Montana was the greatest professional football player I ever saw," said his coach, Bill Walsh.

"I'll say it without disclaimer," said ex-coach and TV analyst John Madden, "this guy is the greatest quarterback who ever played the game."

It seems that destiny preordained that Montana would achieve greatness. He seems to have been born, raised, and groomed for it. Start with his name: *Joe Montana!* No Hollywood screenwriter could concoct a more perfect name for a football hero.

Add to that his upbringing in western Pennsylvania. No part of the country, not even the fabled Southern California and its ballyhooed "quarterback camps" and "football Meccas" in Orange County and the L.A. suburbs, approaches western PA, where the likes of Johnny U., Joe Namath, Jim Kelly, and Dan Marino have slung footballs for the great high school traditions of longtime Friday night fame.

Montana was a great prep signal-caller growing up outside Pittsburgh. He was also an all-state basketball star and a baseball pitcher considered to have big-league potential. A high school legend, he naturally ended up at Notre Dame, but at South Bend his hopes and dreams appeared for a while to have fallen apart.

As a freshman in 1975, Montana found himself relegated deep on the depth chart. Originally recruited by Ara Parseghian, he had been "inherited" by the new coach, Dan Devine, from the Green Bay Packers. A hard-nosed type, Devine was not about to hand over Fighting Irish football to a freshman, regardless of his reputation. That was the *Rudy* team. As a 1976 sophomore,

Montana was frustrated to find that he had not emerged above the other blue-chippers competing for the starting job. When 1977 rolled around, he felt that surely by now he would have his chance, but inconsistency set him back on the bench. Notre Dame had one loss and seemed fairly mediocre when Southern California came to South Bend. The Trojans had been dominating Notre Dame for the past decade, as well as the rest of college football. Devine decided to give Montana his chance, perhaps out of desperation. Another "desperate" move was to outfit his team with green jerseys. When they took the field, the Notre Dame home crowd exploded. Joe rode that momentum, shredding the USC defense in a huge victory.

He was inconsistent at times in later games, but Notre Dame managed to win their remaining contests. Montana was given the start in the Cotton Bowl. No. 5 Notre Dame was a heavy underdog against unbeaten, No. 1–ranked Texas with Heisman running back Earl Campbell.

Montana directed the Irish to victory. Michigan lost in the Rose Bowl, Oklahoma in the Orange Bowl. Montana had led Notre Dame to an improbable national championship.

In 1978 Montana was a Heisman Trophy candidate on a team with repeat national title aspirations. He was at times brilliant, at times inconsistent. His Heisman chances blurred, as did his potential draft status. What he did at season's end, however, was spectacular beyond words. Looking back, it seems impossible to believe that his performance against USC and in the Cotton Bowl against Houston did not propel him to the first round, if not the first pick, but it did not.

Trailing by three touchdowns, he rallied the Irish before a stunned Coliseum crowd, only to see a last-second field goal steal the national title from Notre Dame and give it, eventually, to the Trojans. The 'SC comeback was nothing compared to the Cotton Bowl.

The weather was freezing, with heavy wind chills, ice, and snow stacked on the sideline. Montana had the flu—he carried a high fever, had cold sweats, was on the verge of fainting, and was dizzy. Houston built an enormous lead. At halftime Montana was almost benched, as in hospitalized or at least put to bed. Visions of George Gipp, who died of pneumonia after playing in a freezing game against Michigan State, stirred the Irish soul. Montana came out and led the Irish to an insane come-from-behind win that is one of the most storied in Irish lore.

While Montana was finishing his up-and-down college career, Bill Walsh was on the rise. After two years reviving Stanford football, he was named coach of the 49ers. In the spring of 1979 he presided over his first draft. The first couple of rounds came and went, with a series of quarterbacks, running backs, receivers, linebackers, and linemen chosen by various pro franchises. Sitting in a coffee shop in Manhattan Beach, California, Montana wondered when he would be drafted.

The 49ers were looking for a quarterback. Speculation had it that Walsh would pick Steve Dils, who had enjoyed success under him at Stanford. Instead, Montana was taken with the 82nd pick.

Some said that former 49er John Brodie, also a Stanford alum, had talked Walsh into picking Montana over the local favorite.

"C'mon, are you kidding me?" Walsh asked in mock amazement when posed this question at 49ers headquarters in Santa Clara, California, in April 2001. "I was not gonna pick Steve Dils over Joe Montana. We're talkin' about Joe Montana here."

Whether this is revisionist history or not, in the end Walsh did pick Montana over Dils. By 1980 Montana was starting. Paul Hackett and Walsh were installing the famed West Coast offense. But the 49ers were mediocre. The franchise was bathed in mediocrity. The concept of greatness emerging from this organization, which in recent years had been a laughingstock, seemed an impossibility.

Montana had that Notre Dame polish, to be sure. He was viewed as a winner, but whether he could win in San Francisco looked like a long shot. Furthermore, the 49ers paled in comparison to their traditional rivals. Across the bay, the Oakland Raiders were the "winningest team in pro football." In 1980, as if to show up the Niners, they won the Super Bowl led by a 49ers cast-off, Jim Plunkett.

Then there were the Rams, still in their glory days at the L.A. Coliseum in 1979. They played to huge crowds at the venerable old stadium. Like the Dodgers winning in front of capacity throngs at beautiful Dodger Stadium while the Giants lost before sparse attendance at the ugly Candlestick, so too did the contrast do nothing for the 49ers' image.

It would be an exaggeration to say that Montana and the 49ers made Candlestick look good, but they sure livened up the place. In 1981 Montana and USC alum Ronnie Lott teamed up to lead San Francisco to ultimate victory in the Super Bowl. Images of Candlestick crowds reveal the usual bad hair, bad clothing styles, and overall unimpressive carryover effect from the doldrum 1970s. But suddenly their "loser" fans were bathed in the glory of their team.

As the decade played itself out, and San Francisco rose in stature on the backs of its football team, there was a sense that such wonders were reserved for more traditional "football towns" like Pittsburgh, Green Bay, or Dallas.

Instead, "title town" was now what iconoclastic *San Francisco Chronicle* columnist Herb Caen had dubbed "Baghdad by the Bay." The Raiders? They split for Tinsel Town, leaving the whole Bay Area to the Niners. The Rams? Their longtime tormentors were no patsies, but rather what *L.A. Times* columnist Jim Murray called "an opponent;" strong enough to make the 49ers look good when they beat them, but not able to defeat the Niners.

At the heart of all of it was Joe Montana. He was to San Francisco what Michael Jordan was to Chicago, what Babe Ruth had been to New York. He was young, handsome, an All-American off the field as well as on. He could do no wrong.

In 1981 the 49ers piled up victory after victory. Many kept waiting for the whole thing to fall apart, as surely it would. After all, these were the *49ers*. They had no history, no tradition. But Montana had it—in high school and at Notre Dame. Lott and tight end Charle Young had a tradition of winning at USC. Center Randy Cross had played for great teams at UCLA. Walsh had lifted Stanford from mediocrity to success almost overnight. These men were flush with success.

Joe Montana looks loose and confident during a Super Bowl week practice prior to his—and the 49ers'—first appearance in an NFL title game. A few days later Montana led his team to a 26–21 win over Cincinnati in Super Bowl XVI. Photo courtesy of AP Images.

As the season played itself out and San Francisco kept getting better instead of worse, Montana became larger than life. He found himself on the cover of *Time* magazine and *Sports Illustrated.* The victory over Dallas in the NFC Championship Game was a defining moment for him.

When the game ended, Joe returned to the 49ers' clubhouse and passed out. He had given all he had, but he gathered himself together enough to lead his team to victory over Cincinnati in the Super Bowl.

In 1984 San Francisco was 15–1. Historians generally point to the 1985 Chicago Bears, the unbeaten 1972 Miami Dolphins, and perhaps the 1966 Green Bay Packers as the greatest pro football teams of all time. But the '84 49ers may well have beaten any one of them. With Montana in his prime and at the helm, betting against him would have been as unwise as going against Jordan during the Bulls' great run.

Montana had a team of stars surrounding him. Running backs Wendell Tyler from UCLA and Roger Craig from Nebraska gave the offense much needed diversity. It was a far better team than the 1981 champions, but they also had a target on their backs. They powered through the playoffs and destroyed Dan Marino and Miami in Super Bowl XIX, a "home" game played just down the road from their Santa Clara headquarters, at Stanford Stadium. The score was a convincing 38–16, and an analysis of the game and season makes it difficult to determine that any team was ever better.

By the mid-1980s, Montana was much more than a football star. He was an American idol, married to a stunning blonde actress/model. Injuries slowed Joe and the team for a few seasons, but he secured his place in history, as well as his starting position after Steve Young was acquired, by leading his team to world championships in 1988 and 1989. Nineteen eighty-nine was probably his greatest season, the highlight coming when he led the Niners to a big comeback win over the Rams on *Monday Night Football* at Anaheim.

TRIVIA

What quarterbacks did Joe Montana have to beat out to become a starter at Notre Dame?

Find the answer on page 169.

"This game features perhaps the best team in pro football history," announcer Al Michaels said in that night's introduction, "led by possibly the best quarterback ever, Joe Montana, having maybe his best season."

When Montana had what may have been his greatest game ever that night, it seemed to seal his place in the pantheon.

GOING CAMPING

For many years, the 49ers trained in a little town called Rocklin, California. Rocklin is about two hours east of San Francisco on Interstate 80, about half an hour past Sacramento. Aside from its 49ers legacy, it is little more than a place motorists stop for gas and food while traveling to and from Lake Tahoe. In the summer, when the 49ers trained there, it is extremely hot but not humid. Unlike the Raiders camp in Santa Rosa, a roadhouse town filled with country-western and biker bars, Rocklin offered little opportunity for the 49ers to find trouble.

Against Denver in the Super Bowl, he led San Francisco to an enormous win, and his obvious superiority over John Elway stood out in a glaring manner.

In 1990 San Francisco looked to be better than any previous 49ers team, but incredibly Bill Parcells stopped Joe and his club in the playoffs. The bid for a third straight Super Bowl title, the unprecedented nature of their aspirations, had made that season almost a walk through history; a Canton, Ohio, highlight reel as much as a season. Alas, even the great 49ers and Montana were proved human.

Steve Young did succeed Montana, and proved not as good, but Hall of Fame–worthy himself, which is a statement in and of itself. Montana stands out among the all-time great San Francisco legends. Joe DiMaggio was from the City, but he never played big-league ball there. Willie Mays was not popular at first and never delivered a world championship at home as he had in New York.

Over in the East Bay, of course, Ken Stabler was a hero, as was Reggie Jackson and Catfish Hunter, but none of the A's ever were as popular as players on other teams. Later A's heroes like Mark McGwire and Jose Canseco were flawed, and the Barry Zito–Mark Mulder teams failed to capture brass rings.

This leaves Barry Bonds, a player of incalculable accomplishment who, all else being equal, should be a walking statue. The fact that somebody that good is not particularly popular is a testament to just how unimpressive he is as a man.

In the end, the greatest San Francisco Bay Area sports heroes remain coach Bill Walsh, defensive back Ronnie Lott, and quarterbacks Steve Young and Joe Montana. They exemplified everything that is great, everything that is expected of athlete/celebrities— good character, being team players, clutch performers, and winners, and having extraordinary records that stand up to any greats of the game throughout history.

Of them, Montana towers a little taller. He is the greatest athlete, the biggest hero San Francisco has ever known, and probably ever will know, and the greatest quarterback ever to lace up cleats!

BILL WALSH THE GENIUS

The San Francisco 49ers of the golden 1980s were a team of superlatives. Discussions can be had to "determine" whether they were the greatest dynasty ever—whether Montana was the best of all quarterbacks, Ronnie Lott the game's all-time greatest defensive back, Jerry Rice the finest receiver, and Bill Walsh the best coach.

Walsh as best coach is a tougher argument to make, not because he was not, but because of self-imposed limitations he put on himself. Walsh was always an erudite, articulate Bay Area kind of guy who liked to play tennis, go to the opera, and read about history. He did not fit into the stereotype of the all-consuming football coach, uninterested in any other form of human endeavor. He did not have the intense toughness of Vince Lombardi. He was more likable than Tom Landry.

A closer parallel might come from the basketball world, where Phil Jackson seems to have been a coach who found newer, modern methods to create champions. But Walsh's abrupt retirement after winning the 1989 Super Bowl detracts from the effort to attach "all-time greatest" status to his career. Had he stuck around, he no doubt would have guided his team to a fourth world championship in 1989, maybe a fifth in 1990, a sixth in 1994, and...?

He won three Super Bowls. Pittsburgh's Chuck Noll won four. Noll was a great coach, but Walsh is thought of as more of an

innovator. Tom Landry of Dallas won two and created new para-
digms in the approach to the game, but his Cowboys also went to
the Big Dance three times only to see rival suitors leave with the
prom queen.

The Walsh-Lombardi comparison seems awkward. The Packers
legend won two Super Bowls, but captured what was known as the
"world championship"—the NFL title with no regard for the
status of the emerging AFL—three times before creation of the
AFL-NFL Championship Game in 1967. But Lombardi's methods
were very different from Walsh's, from personality to preparation
and especially to offensive philosophy.

Walsh's role model, and the best comparison, is with the great
Paul Brown, who turned Cleveland into a juggernaut in the 1950s
before Jim Brown's arrival, then made them even better once he
came on the scene. This makes sense because it was under Brown,
where Walsh was an assistant on his staff with the Cincinnati
Bengals, where Walsh cut his teeth.

A native of San Jose, Walsh earned two degrees from San Jose
State before embarking on a coaching career at Fremont's
Washington High School. In the 1960s he coached under Marv
Levy at Cal and John Ralston at Stanford. He joined the Oakland
Raiders, where he learned under the legendary Al Davis.

"Al Davis is a fascinating man, a true football genius who I
admire greatly," said Walsh.

The football stories of the Raiders, Stanford, and the 49ers
might have been different had Walsh not taken over the semipro
San Jose Apaches. Had he stayed at Oakland, Davis may well have
elevated him to the head-coaching position when John Rauch

SOCIAL PROGRESS

Bill Walsh has been described as a Renaissance man. He has always had
social pathos, and in 1987 started the Minority Coaching Fellowship
program. This program is credited with producing his successor at Stanford,
Tyrone Willingham, who later became the coach at Notre Dame. The NFL
adopted Bill's Fellowship program as a league-wide program.

left. Instead, John Madden took over. The Apaches were no great shakes, but Walsh did get a taste of head coaching before returning to the assistant ranks when Brown hired him at Cincinnati. He was credited with turning Sam Wyche into a creditable pro quarterback.

Walsh has given Brown credit, and it has been convenient to say that he learned under a man of Brown's stature, but the Cincinnati years were not easy for Walsh.

"From all I've read about Bill's Cincinnati experience, it must have left a lasting impression on him," said Montana. "He went into the job with a real chance of becoming head coach of the Bengals. Bill was working for Paul Brown...who apparently was getting ready to either retire or move into the front office on a full-time basis. Unfortunately, Bill's job—offensive coordinator—turned out to be more of a curse than a blessing.... We're talking about pure jealousy. Bill was trying hard to make a name for himself, while Paul was hanging on to his own identity as a legend in the game. This caused friction between the two men...the two men ignored each other. The only time they were seen together in public was on the sideline."

Walsh finally got his big break when he took over at Stanford, where he was 17–7 from 1977 to 1978 with wins in the Bluebonnet Bowl and Sun Bowl. In 1979 his 49ers were 2–14, but improvement in 1980 gave hope that Montana's emergence could mean success. Nobody could possibly have predicted the kind of success that followed.

His teams made seven postseason appearances and claimed six NFC West titles, and Walsh was named NFL Coach of the Year twice (1981, 1984). Later, he was named Coach of the Decade for the 1980s.

DID YOU KNOW...

That Washington High School in Fremont, where Bill Walsh got his coaching start, is also the alma mater of Oakland A's Hall of Fame relief ace Dennis Eckersley?

He became the 14th coach elected to the Hall of Fame in 1993, having compiled a .617 percentage (102–63–1) including a 10–4 postseason record.

Walsh went into broadcasting, teaming with Dick Enberg on Notre Dame and NFL telecasts. He returned to Stanford, where in 1992 he led the Cardinal to a 10–3 record, victory over Notre Dame and Penn State in the Blockbuster Bowl, and a top 10 ranking.

Since leaving coaching, he held various front-office positions with the 49ers and in the athletic department at Stanford. He seamlessly straddled affiliation with both the 49ers and Stanford, remaining an icon at both places. It was most appropriate that in the only Super Bowl ever played in the Bay Area, at Stanford Stadium in 1985, it was Walsh who led San Francisco to victory before the "home" crowd.

Walsh has detractors, but it seems that any detraction of him is more jealousy than anything, just as Paul Brown was jealous of the younger man in Cincinnati. The label "Genius" was attached to Walsh, causing some to scoff that he had such great players that any coach could win, as his successor George Seifert was able to do.

But it was Walsh who built the 49ers' destiny from scratch. He did what none before him did, and none who followed was able to carry the franchise on their own as he had. Maybe because he worked under Brown, and had been on the staff under the likes of Marv Levy and Al Davis, Walsh was proprietary when it came to protecting his own reputation.

There have been coaches who worked under him who felt Walsh manipulated his place in history, but the record speaks for itself. Walsh was never mean-spirited, and a number of successful coaches started careers under him. Pete Carroll did not actually coach on Walsh's staff when he was the 49ers' defensive coordinator in 1995, but he was influenced by the Genius, who recognized that Carroll was a special talent.

Others who learned under him include Dennis Green, Ray Rhodes, Jeff Fisher, Sam Wyche, Rod Dowhower, Bruce Coslet, Sherman Lewis, Brian Billick, George Seifert, Jon Gruden, Paul Hackett, and Tom Holmoe. He appeared to be much more generous in helping young assistants who aspired to become head coaches than the old school leader Paul Brown had been.

The media like to talk about "turning points." The turning point in the franchise history of the 49ers, in the career of Bill Walsh, and in the development of Joe Montana may well have occurred on December 7, 1980, at Candlestick Park against the New Orleans Saints. The Niners were out of the running, but instead of playing out the string, they stirred the home crowd with a glorious comeback all the way from a 35–7 deficit to a 38–35 win in overtime. The 1980 squad was only 6–10, but this game and the positive development of Montana, coupled with the drafting of Lott a few months later, gave them hope that in 1981 the team might contend.

It was similar to the 1969 New York Mets, who after years of floundering in last place, felt that they could build on the development of Tom Seaver and Jerry Koosman in 1968, creating a contender in 1969.

It is one thing to contend. It is an entirely different thing to go all the way, as both the 1969 Mets and 1981 49ers did. In both cases, the world championships were among the most improbable in sports history. There is a difference, however. The Mets were a contending team in the years that followed the 1969 season, but never approached their 1969 performance.

The 49ers, on the other hand, improved and went from a surprise winner to a true dynasty. It was not without its bumps and bruises. In 1982 the players struck, breaking up the season. The 49ers never got on track, and it appeared that their 1981 season had been a fluke.

In 1983 they recovered and contended, but Joe Theismann and Washington got hot, stayed that way, and overcame San Francisco to reach the Super Bowl (only to lose to Marcus Allen and the Los Angeles Raiders).

It is also worth noting that Walsh's 49ers did not ascend to great heights in an era in which no contenders emerged to challenge them. In 1981 the Dallas Cowboys, even though Roger Staubach was gone, posed a major challenge. Theismann's Redskins were a powerhouse in 1982 and 1983. In order to capture the 1985 Super Bowl, Walsh's team had to beat Dan Marino and Miami, a team so explosive that many favored them to win.

Legendary head coach Bill Walsh counsels his players during halftime of the September 14, 1980, contest with the Cardinals. Walsh's chalk talk must have worked—San Francisco prevailed 24–14.

In 1985 and 1986 the 49ers were still an excellent team, but the '85 Bears are thought by many to be the finest team of all time. The 1986 New York Giants were a great team. The NFL's second strike in six years helped deflate the value of the 1987 season, but in 1988 and 1989 San Francisco dominated like never before.

Walsh was gone by 1989, but his legacy was carried on. The 1990 49ers may have been the best of all their teams, but Bill Parcells and the Giants had a monster season, stopping them.

Since the merger of the American and National Football Leagues in 1966, and the creation of the American and National Football Conferences in 1970, the AFC has consistently had the better conference. The Dolphins, Steelers, Raiders, Broncos, and Patriots have all been dynasties, some for longer periods of time than others.

ATLANTIC ALLIANCE

Bill Walsh also was instrumental in establishing NFL Europe, which is credited with creating worldwide popularity for pro football while providing many opportunities for players to prove themselves and later make NFL rosters.

In the NFC, only the 49ers and Cowboys have held that kind of place in history. Even the Cowboys' great record is diminished by the fact that they could not beat Pittsburgh. The Los Angeles Rams contended but lost playoff games year after year. Parcells' teams won four years apart. Great NFC teams like the Redskins, the Bears, and the St. Louis Rams were unable to build on championships as Walsh's 49ers did.

"We beat people to the punch," said Walsh. "We established a standard of performance where each man was an extension of his teammates. We prepared for every contingency and throughout all this there was a single thrust—sacrifice for your team, because you infinitely care.

"We took great pride in playing like a 'precision machine.' We weren't obsessed with individually attracting attention. We could thrive in the volatile, sometimes cruel arena of the National Football League with class, dignity, and mutual respect. I take pride in the fact that every man who wore a 49er uniform could be proud of his participation, even if it was a brief training camp episode."

THIS LOTT WAS A PILLAR OF GREATNESS

The Old Testament tells the story of Lot's wife, who, upon escaping from Sodom and Gomorrah, disobeys God by turning to observe the destroyed city. She is turned into a pillar of salt.

The modern Lott, as in Ronnie Lott, was and remains to this day a pillar of *greatness*, a rock upon which all 49ers championship teams and star players can find strength, inspiration, and something to measure themselves against.

Okay, Joe Montana was the greatest of all 49ers—the face of the team, their glamour boy—but Lott was his equal. Whereas

Montana was the best quarterback, Lott was the best defensive back on this, perhaps the best team.

Hopefully 49ers fans savored and respected what they had, because the kind of talent that played before their eyes was once-in-a-lifetime rare. It was a collection of talent, character, and winning attitude that few are ever lucky enough to witness, much less have stay together as this team did.

Lott was not the greatest of all athletes. He was not the biggest, the fastest, or the strongest. What he had, above all else, was a *willingness* to hit that few football players have. The game is, of course, a contact sport, but no matter how tough these gladiators are, they still must adhere to the rules of human psychology. Those rules will always include the axiom: "Avoid pain."

It is one thing to lay a perfect, center-mass hit on an opposing ball carrier. When done correctly, it makes a loud noise, excites the stadium, and lays out the opponent. Like hitting a home run, it is a rare connection with the "sweet spot," and comes with no pain received, only that which is doled out.

But most hits in a football game are not like that. When the other guy knows it is coming, he defends himself. Blockers and other tacklers impede. Over the course of a game, a season, a career, the hits add up, and each one hurts more than the previous one.

Despite this, despite his own human frailties, Lott was willing to hit with full force every time. He called it *Total Impact*, the name of his 1991 book.

"Right before impact, my adrenaline rises," he said. "I can actually feel it surge. I can taste it. An inner force tells me to push harder. Something deep inside says, 'Let everything go into this hit. Bring it from your toes.'"

An athlete can lift weights, he can pop pills, he can run drills, and he can go through utter histrionics—yelling, clawing, pounding—but he cannot be taught to hit like Lott was willing to hit. Surely he had good coaches and the like, but what he brought to the green plains of the Candlestick turf was instinctual, animalistic. He was born to play football.

Lott grew up in Southern California, but not on the sun-swept strands of Beach Boys mythology. His Southern California was more hardscrabble, the sandy canyons east of Los Angeles. Rialto was and is a little blue-collar town in what is known as the Inland Empire, stretching from San Bernardino to Riverside and beyond, from the deserts of Palm Springs and Death Valley to the Arizona border.

Located some 50 miles east of L.A., it is a different world, especially in his day. A fair number of the citizenry work the oilrigs. High school football is taken seriously. The attitude toward sports is more like that in Texas, or the Midwest, than what people think of when they envision laid-back Southern California.

Lott grew up with discipline. He was patriotic, respected the uniform, and toed the line. It stands to reason, since his father was an Air Force officer and his high school was named after Dwight D. Eisenhower. Lott was a spectacular athlete at Eisenhower High. He hit a home run off of Santa Monica's Tim Leary, who later won 17 games for the 1988 world champion Los Angeles Dodgers. He considered basketball his best sport. He was a *Parade* magazine All-American in football.

The football coach at Eisenhower High fired his team up by playing the opening speech from *Patton* before games.

"I can still hear the words of George C. Scott: 'Americans don't tolerate losers,'" recalled Lott. "'You've got to grease the guns with their guts.'"

Prep football was enormously competitive. The game with rival Fontana drew 8,000 people. A loss in his senior year came at the hands of Chaffey High School from Ontario. They featured Anthony Muñoz, Lott's future teammate at USC, an All-Pro with Cincinnati (and twice an opponent again in Super Bowls XVI and XXIII), now a fellow Hall of Famer.

Lott wanted to play for the best, and at that time this meant USC, 'SC, Southern Cal, or Southern California. He was there during a golden age of Trojan football.

"There was a Camelot quality to USC at that time," said his coach, John Robinson.

Lott took over from All-America defensive back Dennis Thurman. As a sophomore in 1978, he anchored a USC defense that bottled up Joe Montana for the better part of three quarters

Hard-hitting Ronnie Lott personified the 49ers' brilliant defenses during the 1980s. The Hall of Fame defensive back is shown in action during a September 1983 game against the Eagles at Candlestick Park.

in the Notre Dame game at the Coliseum. Montana brought the Irish back before USC captured victory on a 37-yard Frank Jordan field goal. When USC defeated Michigan in the Rose Bowl, they secured their third national championship of the decade.

Lott claims that the 1979 Trojans, despite being denied a second straight national title because of a tie with Stanford, were "arguably the greatest college football team of all time."

As a senior captain and All-American, Lott experienced disappointment. USC was hit with NCAA probation, and the game against UCLA, also penalized, was dubbed the "Probation Bowl."

That game featured the two best secondary players in the country, Lott and the Bruins' Kenny Easley. Just as there is a myth that Bill Walsh almost drafted Steve Dils ahead of Joe Montana, so too is there a myth that two years later he came close to choosing Easley over Lott.

"There's no way I was going to take Kenny Easley over Ronnie Lott!" Walsh exclaimed years later. "Are you kidding me?"

Regardless of how close Walsh may have come to turning the 1980s into the Dils-Easley decade, he made the right picks in the form of Montana and Lott. It is also true that for two years, with Walsh in command and Montana assuming controls of the quarterback position, the team finished under .500. It is further true that when Lott arrived in 1981, they immediately became a winner, a champion, a Super Bowl victor. He was the final pillar in their monument.

Lott played cornerback and free safety. He changed the nature of the position. Just as Lawrence Taylor of the New York Giants made the linebacker an all-purpose defender who could morph from an onrushing lineman into an agile pass-interceptor, Lott changed the perception of the safety from a "finesse" player who went for the ball into a field hawk who went for the ball carrier, with everything he had.

Lott explained his ability to hit, and withstand pain, this way:

Engaged in action during a game, I'm lucky, in a sense, because my body will help me deal with pain. My neurological system works on overdrive, secreting hormones to enable my body not only to repair itself but to speed up the healing process. I'm in a survival mode that I call 'fight or flight.' It's my theory that injuries sustained in the early stages of the game hurt more than those that happen after halftime. In the first quarter, there's not as much adrenaline flowing through the blood stream.

If Lott felt more pain early than he did late in games, he was truly unique. Lott won four Super Bowls and made nine Pro Bowl appearances as a 49er. Eventually, he was allowed to leave, just as Montana would be let go. Lott went with the Los Angeles Raiders, where he played in his college stadium, the L.A. Memorial Coliseum. He also played under Pete Carroll with the New York Jets. In 2000 he, Montana, and former 49ers linebacker Dave Wilcox were inducted into the Pro Football Hall of Fame.

Lott maintains a residence in the Bay Area, where he is an entrepreneur. He is regularly interviewed and lends his name to charities. Both the 49ers and USC Trojans jealously hold onto him. He maintains equal loyalty to both organizations, attending Southern Cal games with his son while staying close to the Niners.

SUPER BOWL XXIX: 49ERS 49, CHARGERS 26

In January 1994 Dallas defeated San Francisco 38–21 in the NFC Championship Game.

"That loss catapulted us to the next year, our championship year," recalled quarterback Steve Young. "We could not deal with that loss. It was too devastating. No one talked about it at all. To this day we haven't dealt with it, and it's probably a good thing. In some strange way, we accepted it."

In 1994 San Francisco rolled to an NFL-best 13–3 record. William Floyd was a Rookie of the Year contender, Ricky Watters was an All-Pro running back. They brought in some major stars:

GOIN' HOLLYWOOD

Niners defensive back Tim McDonald was the "model" for the Cuba Gooding Jr. role in the movie *Jerry Maguire*. According to agent Leigh Steinberg, McDonald was asked what motivated him to play football. "The money," replied McDonald, and director Cameron Crowe turned that into the catchphrase, "Show me the money."

Ken Norton Jr. from Dallas, Rickey Jackson, Gary Plummer, free agents Richard Dent and Toi Cook, and of course the great "Neon Deion" Sanders.

At midseason, the 49ers beat Dallas 21–14, propelling a 10-game winning streak, playoff victories over Chicago and Dallas, again at home, and a trip to Miami to face San Diego in the Super Bowl.

It was Young's first Super Bowl as a starter, but he felt no pressure. "Seriously, by the time I'd gone through the whole thing—taking over the quarterback job from Joe Montana—there was no way anything could ever be like that [in terms of intense media pressure]," said Young. "Even the Super Bowl. I'd faced real

Jerry Rice outruns two Chargers defenders en route to a touchdown during San Francisco's 49–26 rout of San Diego in Super Bowl XXIX. Rice had 10 receptions and three touchdowns in the 49ers' victory. Photo courtesy of AP Images.

LOCAL GUY

Niners tight end Brent Jones, Steve Young's best friend on the team, was a local guy from nearby University of Santa Clara, which is not exactly a "football factory."

media pressure before. Talking about football and a big game—that was nothing!"

When the game started, Young hit Rice for a quick-strike touchdown. San Diego went three-and-out. Watters went up the middle for the Niners, there was a short pass to Floyd, and Young scrambled for 21 yards to midfield. Watters then caught a pass at the Chargers' 30, evaded tacklers, and at 14–0 the game was all over but the shouting.

San Diego managed to score, but the 49ers responded with an impressive drive and scoring pass to Floyd. A deflected punt later gave San Francisco the ball in Chargers territory. Young maneuvered the offense inside the 10, then hit Watters on a short pass, 28–7. It was 28–10 at the half, with the TV audience rapidly decreasing in market share.

San Francisco was virtually perfect. They suffered no turnovers and only 18 yards in penalties. In the second half, Young passed them within sight of the goal, where Watters ran in for their only rushing score. Rice would finish with three TDs.

Young's fifth touchdown pass made the score 42–10. Number six was a quick slant to Rice in the fourth quarter. Young broke Montana's record for TD passes in a Super Bowl, set five years earlier. The 49ers' defense intercepted Chargers quarterback Stan Humphries twice and his backup Gale Gilbert once.

Just as Young had replaced Montana late in the Super Bowl blowout of Denver, Elvis Grbac replaced Young while he and his teammates whooped it up on the sideline.

"After the game, in the locker room, everybody was ecstatic," recalled Young. "I can't describe the feeling."

THE BAD

IT IS DARKEST JUST BEFORE THE DAWN

Cliché time: it is darkest just before the dawn. Richard Nixon: "To appreciate what it is like to be on the highest mountaintop, one must tread through the lowliest valley."

For the San Francisco 49ers, the period from 1973 to 1980 represented the longest, darkest night of their history—a period in which the team tread in the "lowliest valley." The 49ers were born into the old All-American Football Conference as part of the post–World War II expansion. They were adopted into the National Football League in the 1950 season. The Cleveland Browns (now the Baltimore Ravens, not to be confused with the new Cleveland Browns), another AAFC team, was immediately successful. The 49ers were not, but they were competitive.

They had a good season in 1957. In the 1960s the Rams dominated, but San Francisco fielded entertaining teams with star-quality players like John Brodie, Jimmy Johnson, and Dave Wilcox.

From 1970 to 1972, San Francisco had playoff teams, but after the disastrous fourth-quarter loss against Dallas in the first round in '72, they got old, discouraged, and bad...fast.

From 1973 to 1979, San Francisco was terrible. Only the birth of the expansion Tampa Bay Buccaneers prevented them from being the worst team in the league, but even Tampa Bay under coach John McKay rose to the NFC title game by 1979. The 49ers stayed mired in mediocrity.

San Francisco was a failed team. Their young players did not develop. Veterans came in by trade, only to show their age. What made the period even more galling was that it represented a golden era in the league and in the state. San Francisco's failure was accentuated by the fact that their rivals attained the heights of glory.

New Yorkers speak wistfully of the 1950s, when three super-star center fielders—Willie Mays of the Giants, Mickey Mantle of the Yankees, and Duke Snider of the Dodgers—roamed outfield pastures. Rivalries were intense in baseball. Frank Gifford's New York Giants enjoyed a strong football run. But New York cannot compare to what happened in the Golden State from the 1960s until the 1990s.

Obviously this period encompasses 49ers greatness. There were the three division titles of the early 1970s and the five Super Bowl titles of the 1980s and '90s. The Giants were strong in the 1960s. The Angels contended in the 1980s. The Rams were excellent, for the most part, in the 1960s and '70s. Stanford went to two Rose Bowls (1970 and 1971). The Chargers of Dan Fouts were a high-powered early '80s offense.

But the proverbial "glory days" are centered in the 1970s. The cross-bay Raiders were dominant in the 1960s, more dominant in the 1970s and 1980s. USC football was probably as strong from 1962 to 1981 as any collegiate power in history. Their best teams were in the 1970s. UCLA basketball under John Wooden (1964–1975) put together a string like no other, highlighted by an 88-game winning streak in the '70s. The Lakers were contenders in the 1960s, champions in the 1970s, a dynasty in the 1980s. The Golden State Warriors won the 1975 NBA title. The Dodgers were terrific in the 1960s, 1970s, and 1980s. Then there were the Oakland Athletics. While the 49ers stumbled and bumbled, the A's put together one of the greatest sports dynasties in history. All these champions relegated the Niners to the back of the newspapers.

In addition to all these great teams, the 1970s saw a rise in California prep, junior college, and "other" sports. Redwood High

SO CLOSE AND YET SO FAR

After winning three straight division titles, there was still hope that Dick Nolan's team could continue to hold their own, and that the transition from John Brodie to Steve Spurrier would be a winning one. It was looking good in the second half of the first game of the 1973 season, when the 49ers were threatening to end world champion Miami's winning streak. But in searing heat and humidity before 68,275, the Dolphins recovered to win 21–13. Their 18-game streak was ended the following week at Cal's Memorial Stadium in a 12–7 loss to Oakland, not played in the Coliseum because the A's had a game that Sunday.

of Marin County and Lakewood High of L.A. County had dynasties in baseball. Verbum Dei of Los Angeles rose to unprecedented prep basketball heights. High school football in the Southland took on a new status above and beyond Texas, Ohio, and Pennsylvania. Cerritos Junior College enjoyed a baseball run like none ever seen, and Fullerton College was a junior college football powerhouse. Stanford tennis became a juggernaut. USC and UCLA track dominated (Cal won the 1970 NCAA track title before losing it to academic ineligibility). Had USC or UCLA been countries, they would have been among the top medal winners at the 1976 Montreal Olympics. USC baseball captured five straight College World Series titles. After Title IX, women's sports took a giant leap forward, with California becoming the trendsetter.

The mid- to late 1970s were tough times in San Francisco, however. Greatness abounded all around them—across the bay and in hated Los Angeles. But the Giants and 49ers represented mediocrity. Candlestick Park, not yet 20 years old, was immediately declared ancient, dirty, a symbol of all things second-rate, low-rent, unimpressive.

The Oakland–Alameda County Coliseum was considered more comfortable, fan-friendly, and accessible. The adjacent Coliseum Arena was modern and filled to capacity. Down south, Trojans, Bruins, and Rams games at the Coliseum were played

Steve Spurrier—shown in action against the Eagles in December 1973—was the heir-apparent to 49ers quarterback John Brodie. Injuries felled Spurrier in 1974, and San Francisco found itself in a long slump that was finally halted by Bill Walsh and Joe Montana in 1981.

before enormous throngs at a stadium considered a shrine of immortality. Anaheim Stadium and San Diego Stadium were modern marvels. The Fabulous Forum was home to Hollywood's "in" crowd. Dodger Stadium was the Taj O'Malley.

Then there was San Francisco itself. The city was dirty, corrupt, seemingly taken over by organized crime and peep show booths. Tourists found other, better destinations. Homeless were camped out on the streets, at city hall, and in front of restaurants that patrons chose not to patronize. Once a vibrant city famous for its wild celebrations at the end of World War II—a favorite of sailors and other servicemen—San Francisco by the 1970s was a moribund hangover in the aftermath of the drug-addled Summer of Love, the hippie revolution, the dropout generation, and the protest movement. The fan base at Candlestick was not generally *from* San Francisco, anyway. Their people came from the suburbs of Marin, San Mateo, and Santa Clara counties. The teams they fielded gave them little incentive to drive through dangerous Bayview streets, leaving their parked cars to the tender mercies of tire thieves and vandals. There was certainly nothing worth doing after the game near Candlestick, and little incentive to venture into the heart of the City itself.

Amidst this desultory atmosphere, a football team lived down to expectations. Nineteen seventy-three marked the end of John Brodie's and defensive tackle Charlie Krueger's careers. Injuries killed the club in a 5–9 year against the league's toughest schedule. Center Forrest Blue and linebacker Dave Wilcox were rare bright spots, both voted All-Pro. Tight end Ted Kwalick out of Penn State was a top performer. That year the Rams made a big comeback. New coach Chuck Knox installed a conservative, ground-oriented offense around the experienced veteran John Hadl, obtained from San Diego when San Francisco native Dan Fouts took over. Los Angeles was 12–2. The Rams' success symbolized the difference between the two cities. L.A. was the "city of the future," hailed as innovative in the arts and technology, a place that supposedly had "gotten it right" in terms of harmonious race relations.

In 1974 the Niners' heir apparent quarterback Steve Spurrier was injured, and his four replacements failed to make the grade. After opening with two hopeful wins, they dropped seven straight in a 6–8 year. One bright spot was Rookie of the Year Wilbur Jackson. Jackson is a historic figure. He was the first full-scholarship African American player ever recruited by Bear Bryant at the University of Alabama. In order to "grease the skids" for Jackson's acceptance, Bryant scheduled a game against integrated powerhouse Southern California in 1970. When the Trojans won big at Legion Field, 'Bama fans were clamoring for fast black players...like Wilbur Jackson. By the time his Crimson Tide career was over, Jackson had been voted team captain, and the South had risen again.

"Football's religion in the South," said Jackson. "When I got out to California, I heard about the Big Game [Cal versus Stanford]. I checked it out. It wasn't like any game in the SEC in terms of excitement. Fans out there were laid-back, but I enjoyed my time in the Bay Area."

Dave Wilcox finally had to retire when a knee injury ended his excellent career. The Rams again won the Western Division, but the balance of power had shifted well in favor of the American Football Conference, winners of eight of 10 Super Bowls in the decade.

In 1975 the Rams were a dominant defensive team, but Dallas ended their momentum in the NFC title game at the Coliseum. San Francisco was an afterthought at 5–9, although their 24–23 win over L.A. ended an embarrassing 10-game losing streak to the Rams.

New coach Monte Clark seemed to have turned things around in 1976 (8–6). Enormous hopes were pinned on quarterback Jim Plunkett. A local product from James Lick High School in San Jose, Plunkett captured the 1970 Heisman Trophy at Stanford. After leading the Indians to a Rose Bowl upset of Ohio State, he was selected with the first overall pick of the 1971 NFL Draft by New England.

In his first game at Foxboro Stadium, Plunkett engineered a victory over the mighty Oakland Raiders, but went downhill after that, losing his job to Steve Grogan. Still youthful, the move to San Francisco seemed a natural fit for Plunkett, and indeed in 1976 improvement was made. But after a 6–1 start that had everybody excited, the Niners tanked.

Running back Del Williams rushed for 1,203 yards, and UCLA center Randy Cross made the All-Rookie team. The great Jimmy Johnson retired after 16 years. A four-game losing streak ended playoff hopes and left Plunkett subject to much criticism. The Rams again captured the West, but even worse, the cross-bay Raiders finally broke through after years of dominant, yet ultimately disappointing seasons to capture the Super Bowl, which was played in Pasadena sunshine.

In 1977 Eddie DeBartolo Jr. bought the team and brought in Joe Thomas as general manager. There was little indication that this would improve things as the club lost their first five in a 5–9 campaign under new coach Ken Meyer. But there were indications—in faraway places—that something new was in the air. Halfway across the country, junior quarterback Joe Montana led Notre Dame first to a green-shirt upset of Southern California, then to a Cotton Bowl win over Earl Campbell's Texas Longhorns, en route to the national championship.

Closer to home, a short drive down Highway 101, the former coach at Washington High in Fremont, who had been an assistant under Marv Levy at Cal, under John Ralston at Stanford, under Al Davis in Oakland, and under Paul Brown at Cincinnati, finally got his chance as a head man. His name was Bill Walsh. When he returned Stanford to respectability after a few down years, people started to take notice of his "new ideas."

Nineteen seventy-eight was the nadir of the decade. Plunkett was discarded like stale French bread, but hope was placed on another local legend. Orenthal James Simpson grew up in the Potrero Hill section of San Francisco. He prepped at Galileo High, then set every junior college record imaginable at City College. At USC, his legend was made: a national championship and a Heisman. National icon status came to him in Buffalo, where the first overall pick of the 1969 draft broke Jim Brown's single-season rushing record, becoming the first ever to gain 2,000 yards in 1973. In his prime, O.J.

DID YOU KNOW...

That Monte Clark, who coached in San Francisco for one year (1976), had been a star player at the University of Southern California?

had many pundits contemplating whether he indeed had replaced Brown as the greatest football player ever. While he probably fell just short of that, O.J. was a hero and major superstar, and not just on the field—he was a movie star, a commercial spokesman, and the most popular sports figure in the pre–Michael Jordan era.

He was brought home to San Francisco in 1978 and was joined in 1979 by his Potrero Hill, Galileo, CCSF, USC, and Buffalo Bills

WINNERS

There were good players on the bad 49ers teams of the mid-1970s. Wide receiver Gene Washington had been one of Jim Plunkett's targets at Stanford. Tight end Ted Kwalick was a former All-American at Penn State. Defensive end Cedrick Hardman and center Woody Peoples were All-Pros. Defensive tackle Charlie Krueger was a picture of the tough pro football player.

teammate Al Cowlings. O.J. was well past his prime, however. He was cheered, but offered no magic in a 2–14 season. Failed coach Pete McCulley was let go, and the decision was made: a youth movement; a new direction; no more failed, injured veterans. O.J. hung up his cleats, heading to Hollywood and an unfortunate destiny.

This meant two things. First, Walsh was hired after leading Stanford to a bowl win and two strong seasons. Then Walsh drafted Montana, still available—*incredibly*—in the third round. He considered his own Stanford signal-caller, Steve Dils, but was impressed by Montana's winning ways at Notre Dame.

Walsh installed a high-powered passing scheme, and quarterback Steve DeBerg was effective with Montana learning the ropes behind him, but their 2–14 record had nobody thinking that greatness lay just around the corner.

In 1980 progress was sure. They started out strong and finished strong in a 6–10 year. Wide receiver Dwight Clark had with 82 catches. Montana took over as the starter and completed 65 percent of his passes. Heading into 1981, the 49ers were hopeful. Nobody could predict anything like what would transpire in that and subsequent seasons, but one thing seemed apparent: after a long, black night, the first dawn of a new day was peeking over the horizon.

GALE SAYERS RUNS WILD IN THE MUD

Gale Sayers is a Hall of Fame running back who probably is more famous for things he accomplished in a shorter period of time than any other pro football player.

Sayers, an African American who grew up in Omaha but somehow eluded Nebraska recruiters, took his skills to the University of Kansas, where he achieved All-America status. In 1965 he was the prized rookie of George Halas' Chicago Bears. That year, the Bears brought in an unheralded rookie running back from Wake Forest named Brian Piccolo.

Piccolo was white, from the South, and competed for Sayers' position. Nevertheless, they became good friends. Piccolo later died of cancer. The friendship between the two men, and Sayers' impassioned love of Piccolo, was embodied by his memorial words, "I am third," a reference to Piccolo and God coming ahead of him. *I Am Third* was the title of Sayers' book and the inspiration for a well-done movie, *Brian's Song*, starring James Caan and Billy Dee Williams.

Sayers burst upon the pro football scene in 1965. In his first heavy preseason action, he raced 77 yards on a punt return, 93 yards on a kickoff return, and then startled everyone with a 25-yard scoring pass against the Los Angeles Rams.

In the regular season, he scored four touchdowns, including a 96-yard game-breaking kickoff return, against the Minnesota Vikings. On December 12, 1965, Sayers squared off against the 49ers on a muddy Wrigley Field. That afternoon, he tied an NFL record when he scored six touchdowns in the Bears' 61–20 victory.

Included in his sensational spree were an 80-yard pass-run play, a 50-yard rush, and a 65-yard punt return. His performance was particularly startling because of the field conditions. Somehow he was able to make cuts and pivots in the muck, while

SOLDIER FIELD VERSUS KEZAR STADIUM

Both stadiums have hosted high school, college, and pro football. Soldier Field at one time held 120,000 and was filled to capacity when USC played Notre Dame in front of the largest crowd of all time in 1927. The Bears also played in a baseball stadium—Wrigley Field—just as the 49ers, after leaving Kezar, played in a baseball stadium, Candlestick Park.

TOP 10 49ERS NEMESES

1. Roger Staubach, Dallas Cowboys
2. Troy Aikman, Dallas Cowboys
3. Lawrence Taylor, New York Giants
4. Fred Dryer, L.A. Rams
5. Bobby Layne, Detroit Lions
6. Brett Favre, Green Bay Packers
7. Mike Singletary, Chicago Bears
8. Emmitt Smith, Dallas Cowboys
9. Duane Thomas, Dallas Cowboys
10. Elroy "Crazy Legs" Hirsch, L.A. Rams

San Francisco defenders fell all over themselves.

Gale scored 22 touchdowns and 132 points, both then-rookie records.

Quiet, unassuming, and always ready to compliment a teammate for a key block, Sayers continued to sizzle in 1966, 1967, and well into the 1968 season. Then, in the ninth game, Sayers suffered a knee injury that required immediate surgery. It was a San Francisco player, Kermit Alexander, who cut Sayers down, rupturing his cartilage.

After a tortuous rehabilitation program, Sayers came back in 1969 in spectacular manner, winding up with his second 1,000-yard rushing season and universal Comeback Player of the Year honors. But injuries continued to take their toll and, just before the 1972 season, Sayers finally had to call it quits. His knee problems ultimately made it impossible for him to do what he did best; those exquisite cuts and pivots, as if on a dime.

In his relatively short career, he compiled a record that can never be forgotten. His totals show 9,435 combined net yards, 4,956 yards rushing, and 336 points scored. At the time of his retirement, Sayers was the NFL's all-time leader in kickoff returns. He won All-NFL honors five straight years and was named Offensive Player of the Game in three of the four Pro Bowls in which he played.

T.O. THE WHINER

Terrell Owens is probably not as bad a guy as some make him out to be, but he sure makes it hard to believe otherwise. How good is he? From a strictly physical standpoint, his ability is world-class, but his off-field (and on-field) antics prove that distractions can indeed take away from a player's contributions.

A few years ago he appeared in a pregame skit that "shocked" viewers watching *Monday Night Football*. In an ABC ploy meant to advertise football and the then-upcoming hot series *Desperate Housewives*, blonde bombshell Nicollette Sheridan appears wearing a towel and a lustful expression, all alone in the locker room, except for T.O. She tempts T.O. not to go out and play football, the implication obviously being that wild times are to be had with her, *sans* the robe which is shown falling to the floor.

What all of this says is not clear. T.O. shrugged off the sideline pundits and went on his merry way, which included on-field highlights, commercial endorsements, and notoriety. He has never really *hurt* anybody, although he has certainly set a few football teams back when they needed him to buckle down. Nobody would begrudge him the money he makes or the fame and fans he enjoys.

As of this point in T.O.'s career, his can be judged to be one filled with many exciting highlights, but ultimately he is viewed negatively. As great as he is, he has played on teams that might have gone all the way, or at least further than they did. T.O.'s disruptive ways are, in the end, one of the reasons some of those teams failed. In a team game, this is not a good legacy.

Like Randy Moss, T.O. must lead a team to a Super Bowl championship in order to completely shed his image. Until then, rightly or wrongly, he will be viewed as a player who helped get teams close to the title, then prevented those teams from attaining the title. A one-time teammate and semi-adversary, Donovan McNabb, on the other hand, is viewed as a guy who gave every measure of himself to help his team win. Receivers like Fred Biletnikoff and Jerry Rice and quarterbacks like Ken Stabler and Joe Montana are players who are viewed as winners who went beyond their natural abilities. T.O. is heretofore viewed as wasting his many gifts.

T.O. was the first son of Marilyn Heard. Most of Marilyn's childhood was spent in fear and silence. Marilyn's mother, Alice, was cruel to her children, raising them in a confined environment with little love or support. Marilyn wasn't allowed to play with other children, and had to come home directly after school. If she didn't, she would pay the price.

Marilyn had Terrell when she was 17 years old. A neighbor 14 years her senior, L.C. Russell, who lived across the street with his wife and kids, was the baby's father. After Terrell, Marilyn had a girl named Latasha. She was married to the infant's father for a brief time. Then in the early 1980s came two more babies, Sharmaine and Victor, fathered by another man.

Terrell often stayed with his grandmother Alice. He was whipped regularly. For all the abuse, however, he loved Alice, viewing her as a second mother. Alice's marriage fell apart, and she drank heavily. Terrell was forced to watch out for her. One time Alice was so intoxicated, she put her purse in the oven and burned all her money. She bought Terrell a go-cart, but they recklessly drove on the highway.

When Terrell turned 12, he befriended a girl across the street. Her father noticed and confronted him, warning Terrell that the girl was actually his half-sister. Thus the youngster learned who his father was.

Terrell loved football, idolizing San Francisco star Jerry Rice. Alice opposed his playing, but Marilyn supported him. Marilyn

DADDY DEAREST

Dennis Erickson was once a golden boy, but his story is indicative of how the coaching game can take strange twists and turns of fate. Erickson succeeded Jimmy Johnson as coach at the University of Miami, winning a national championship in 1991. He led Oregon State to the Fiesta Bowl, where the 11–1 Beavers trounced Notre Dame. When the USC job became vacant, Erickson was the top choice of athletics director Mike Garrett. He turned down what was traditionally one of the most prestigious jobs in the profession. Since that time, Pete Carroll (Garrett's third or fourth choice) is being compared to John McKay and Howard Jones. Erickson had zero success with the 49ers, was fired, and had zero success at Idaho, where his salary was a fraction of what he made in his heyday. But he has enjoyed some winning seasons at Arizona State. He is a mercenary.

often found herself back in Alice's house with Terrell, but she eventually moved into a beat-up two-bedroom home. Terrell stayed with Alice because there simply wasn't room for him in the cramped dwelling.

At Benjamin Russell High School, Terrell lettered four times in football and track, accumulated three letters in basketball, and one in baseball. He actually didn't start for the football team until his senior year. He even thought about quitting the sport, but his coaches talked him out of it. He had great, untapped ability.

Tall, lanky, and fast, Terrell's skills were overlooked, but the University of Tennessee at Chattanooga went after the multisport star. With the Moccasins, Terrell lined up at forward on the basketball team for three years, including five starts for the UTC squad that qualified for the NCAA tournament in 1995. In his senior year, he anchored the school's 4 x 100 relay team.

In football he wore No. 80 in honor of Jerry Rice. His biggest day came against Marshall, when he set a school record with four TDs. He caught 58 receptions for 836 yards and six touchdowns, earning second-team All–Southern Conference honors. He was regularly double-covered as a senior and had a less stellar season: 43 receptions for 666 yards and a touchdown.

At 6'3" and more than 200 pounds with speed, Terrell was drafted by San Francisco in the third round (89th overall) of the 1996 draft. The 49ers had traded up to pick J.J. Stokes out of UCLA the year before, but he disappointed. It was a chance to play with Rice and quarterback Steve Young.

George Seifert was the head coach. Pete Carroll was the defensive coordinator. Bill Walsh returned to the front office. The team appeared to be a Super Bowl contender. Defensively, Bryant Young was among the league's best on the line, while Tim McDonald and Merton Hanks were solid at the safety positions.

When Stokes went down with an injury, Terrell caught four passes for 94 yards against Cincinnati, including a 45-yard touchdown. In the final 10 games, he posted 32 receptions for 488 yards and four touchdowns. The Niners finished second in the NFC West at 12–4. Young suffered two concussions. In the playoffs, they were beaten by Brett Favre and the Green Bay Packers.

Seifert retired and was replaced by Steve Mariucci. Carroll took over as the head coach at New England. Young was turning 36, and Rice would soon be 35. Running back Garrison Hearst was brought in. On defense, the front seven was strong, but the secondary was average.

Injuries to Rice and Young increased the focus on Terrell, and San Francisco started 11–1. The defense responded, too. Owens became most dangerous after catching the ball with 60 receptions for 936 yards and eight touchdowns.

San Francisco finished 13–3, good for first in the NFC West. In the playoffs, they beat Minnesota 38–22. Owens, Rice, and Stokes matched the Vikings' Randy Moss, Cris Carter, and Jake Reed. The Packers, however, defeated them 23–10 in the NFC Championship Game. It was their fourth defeat in the last three years versus Green Bay. Terrell caught six balls for 100 yards.

In 1998 Rice returned, Mariucci promised to open up the passing attack, Dana Stubblefield left via free agency, while Bryant Young and Junior Bryant were still a terrific duo up front. In the defensive backfield, R.W. McQuarters, San Francisco's first-round pick from Oklahoma State, looked to settle in at one of the corners.

The 49ers started strong with wins in their first three games and ranked first in the NFL in rushing and passing. Terrell became a star. He escorted Hearst into the end zone on a 96-yard touchdown run for an overtime victory over the New York Jets. Two months later, he led the Niners over the Giants, hauling in a 79-yard touchdown pass, while Hearst rushed for 166 yards.

Trailing Green Bay 27–23 in the playoffs, Steve Young guided the Niners downfield, and with three seconds left, he crouched under center for a final snap from the Packers' 25-yard line. After tripping over a teammate's foot, he spotted Terrell near the goal line and fired a strike. Terrell got hammered as the ball reached him, and he somehow managed to hold on to deliver a thrilling 30–27 win. The Falcons, however, beat them 20–18 and ended up in the Super Bowl.

In 1999 the team signed running backs Charlie Garner and Lawrence Phillips and also added Charles Haley to bolster the defense. But Young was out with a series of concussions, and Rice's

Terrell Owens is distraught on the 49ers' bench in the closing moments of a December 1996 defeat at the hands of the Panthers. An Owens bobble resulted in a drive-killing interception by Carolina that secured a 30–24 win.
Photo courtesy of AP Images.

yards-per-catch dipped to a career low. Mariucci turned to quarterbacks Jeff Garcia and Steve Stenstrom. After a 3–1 start, they dropped eight straight, ending 4–12. Owens had 60 receptions for 754 yards and four touchdowns. Young announced his retirement, leaving the team to Garcia.

Ahmed Plummer from Ohio State and Jason Webster from Texas A&M joined the defensive unit. Early in the 2000 campaign, the Niners visited Dallas. San Francisco jumped out to a big lead and built it further on a touchdown pass to Terrell. Unable to control his emotions, he sprinted to the star in the middle of the field in a celebration that clearly offended the Cowboys. When Terrell scored again and repeated his actions, some on the opposing sideline had seen enough, including George Teague, who blindsided the San Francisco receiver.

Thus was "T.O." born.

The 49ers suspended T.O. for a week and fined him $24,000. He reacted angrily. The media savaged him. National sportstalk host Jim Rome made blistering fun of T.O.'s "star" turn. The team went downhill fast. Rice was showered with praise and ovations, in contrast to the treatment accorded T.O. But T.O. stole the show. Running free all day long, he logged an NFL-record 20 receptions for 283 yards against Chicago. T.O. finished the 2000 season with 97 receptions and 1,451 yards, scoring 13 touchdowns. Terrell earned a trip to Hawaii for his first Pro Bowl. Garcia blossomed, too.

Still vilified in the press, T.O. began to feud with Mariucci in 2001 after Jerry Rice left to become an Oakland Raider. Teammates avoided him in the locker room.

When San Francisco blew a 19-point lead in Chicago—losing in overtime after T.O. mishandled a pass that Bears free safety Mike Brown intercepted and returned for the game-winning score—he accused Mariucci of protecting good friend Dick Jauron, the Chicago head coach whose job was on the line. The comment left people to ponder two possibilities. One: that it was a stupid comment. Two: that T.O. might actually be, simply, stupid. Neither possibility served him publicly. It definitely was of no value in his relations with the coach.

The Niners still finished 12–4. T.O. recorded 93 receptions for 1,412 yards and 16 touchdowns. He was selected to the Pro Bowl

THE UGLY

Denise DeBartolo York and Dr. John York are not the worst owners in pro football history, it just seems that way. Denise's brother, Eddie, took over a bad franchise and helped turn them into the greatest dynasty pro football has ever known. Denise and her husband, York, then put a power play together. True, it was not as bad as what allegedly went down with Georgia Frontiere, taking the Rams from Carroll Rosenbloom and stealing it from his son, but the DeBartolo-York combo is, well, unimpressive. In their tenure they have overseen the transformation of the greatest dynasty ever into one of the worst eras in 49ers history.

for the second time and earned first-team All-Pro honors from the Associated Press, but San Francisco lost to old nemesis Green Bay 25–15 in the playoffs. T.O. caught just four passes, and a ball that would have given San Francisco a lead was tipped away. In the locker room, center Jeremy Newberry overheard T.O. openly complain and advised him to keep quiet. T.O.'s response: demand a trade.

In the off-season, with no trade in the offing, Mariucci tried to patch things up. Playing in Seattle in a key 2002 division showdown, T.O. hauled in the game-winning touchdown in the 28–21 victory. Then he pulled a Sharpie out of his sock, signed the ball, and handed it to his financial adviser sitting in an end zone luxury suite rented by Shawn Springs, the cornerback he had just beaten. America was unimpressed. Seahawks coach Mike Holmgren said he dishonored the game. ESPN analysts Sean Salisbury, Dennis Green, and Tom Jackson ripped him. T.O.'s reaction: to bring a camera crew into his home like a rap star showing off his "crib." America was less impressed. T.O.'s reaction: to blame his unpopularity on racism. America's conclusion: T.O. is either an idiot or doing an excellent imitation of one.

On the field he was spectacular, at least as a regular-season player in games that did not mean everything: a career-high 100 receptions, 1,300 yards, and 13 touchdowns. The Niners went 10–6, finishing first in the weak NFC West.

Down by 14 points at halftime against the Giants in the first playoff game, T.O. started spouting off. They fell further behind, 38–14. But T.O. showed leadership, reeling in nine passes for 177 yards and two touchdowns, plus a pair of two-point conversions. San Francisco won 39–38 in miraculous fashion.

Then Tampa Bay crushed them 31–6. Mariucci was fired. Dennis Erickson, who had turned down the USC job in 2000, leaving it open to the third or fourth choice (Pete Carroll), was brought in. After a loss to Minnesota, T.O. went into a screaming rage. He made the Pro Bowl with 80 receptions, 1,102 yards, and nine touchdowns. Mainly he spouted off about how unhappy he was. Nobody was impressed with anything about him at this point other than his God-given abilities.

DID YOU KNOW...

That Alex Smith, San Francisco's No. 1 draft pick in 2005, played at Helix High School in San Diego, where he was a teammate of Reggie Bush's? Utah's Smith, USC's Bush and Matt Leinart, and Oklahoma's Adrian Petersen and Jason White were all finalists for the 2004 Heisman Trophy. The only reason Bush did not make two straight Helix High No. 1 picks in 2006 was because of a last-second question about a house owned by his parents. He went No. 2 to New Orleans. Hall of Fame basketball star Bill Walton also led Helix to a state record for consecutive victories in 1970 that was broken in the early 1980s by Drake High of San Anselmo.

He was traded to Baltimore. Infuriated, he forced a settlement in which he ended up at Philadelphia in a three-way deal including the Ravens. He confirmed the low opinion of his moral character when he complained during the preseason about not seeing the ball enough, and in an interview with *Playboy* hinted that Jeff Garcia was gay. Garcia subsequently dated a *Playboy* Playmate.

T.O.'s actions in Philadelphia were moronic, starting with *actually arriving late for the first game.* In the volatile Philly atmosphere, T.O. played spectacularly on the field.

Against the Bears, T.O. did six sit-ups for each of his TD catches to that point in the season. Cleveland fans rained disrespect on T.O., causing him to tear down signs berating him. In a 15–10 win over Baltimore, he mocked Ray Lewis' "Squirrel" dance, gyrating in the end zone after a touchdown that put the contest on ice.

T.O. touched off a firestorm of controversy with the racy television promotion with Nicollette Sheridan. Ultimately, amid league pressure, Terrell apologized, as did ABC and Sheridan.

Then T.O. suffered an injury prior to the playoffs. Quarterback Donovan McNabb led them to a 27–14 win over Minnesota. T.O. was unavailable in that and the NFC Championship Game win over Atlanta. Donovan showed he was the team leader and Philly did not need T.O.

T.O. played fairly well in the Super Bowl, but his injury ultimately may have made the difference in the 24–21 loss to Tom Brady and New England.

After the Super Bowl, he dumbly criticized everybody and everything. He had reached new heights of selfish egotism. Eventually, despite obvious talent, the decision was made that his character faults overshadowed his ability. He was run out of Philly on a rail and ended up in Dallas and then Buffalo, where he continued to say and do ignorant things.

THE UGLY

A BLACK DAY BY THE BAY

The date was December 23, 1972; a date that will live in infamy in the San Francisco Bay Area. That year, 1972, was star-crossed in many ways. In the spring the baseball players had struck, interrupting the beginning of the season. The gaudy, hairy Oakland A's still managed to win the American League West, then captured thrilling playoff and World Series victories over Detroit and Cincinnati to deliver the first professional world championship to Northern California.

In September everything that could go wrong went terribly wrong when sports and politics met in an ugly confrontation at the Munich Olympics. Palestinian terrorists murdered Israeli athletes. Then the Soviet Union literally stole the gold medal from the United States in basketball. Bay Area swimmer Rick DeMont had his gold medal taken from him because his asthma medication was on the banned substance list, which had been updated after the original list—one that did not include his medication—had been submitted to his coaches.

Richard Nixon won by the largest margin in presidential history that fall, but his Watergate imbroglio was already a done deal waiting to be exposed by the *Washington Post*.

Football was successfully played on both sides of the bay by respective division champions Oakland and San Francisco. The dream of a Bay Bridge Super Bowl just 400 miles down the road, at the Los Angeles Memorial Coliseum, gave hope to many. The same prospect hung in the air two years earlier, only to be dashed when the Raiders lost at Baltimore and Dallas upended the 49ers at Kezar Stadium in the conference championship games.

The odds were not in favor of the two teams. Miami was unbeaten, a team for the ages that would have to be overcome in the AFC. In the NFC a more egalitarian landscape prevailed. Dallas was the defending Super Bowl winner but strangely inconsistent in '72.

On December 23, fans were hoping for early Christmas presents. What at first appeared to be shiny toys for both clubs turned out to be lumps of coal. Such hope there was at first—a great day of football viewing with logs burning in the fireplace, the smell of holiday smoke emanating from neighborhood chimneys, packages under trees, friends and family gathered for holiday good cheer.

With morning coffee came Oakland at Pittsburgh. It was one of those nerve-wracking defensive struggles, with the young Steelers, led by Terry Bradshaw, clinging to a 6–0 fourth-quarter lead over the veteran Raiders. Then Ken Stabler, a legend in the making whose star would shine almost as brightly as Montana's, ran 30 yards for the go-ahead score.

Bradshaw went to the well three times with nothing to show for it, leaving fourth-and-desperation with a few seconds left. His pass bounced off either Frenchy Fuqua, Jack Tatum, or both of them simultaneously, landing in the hands of Franco Harris just inches above the ground. His "Immaculate Reception" resulted in a touchdown and a 13–7 Pittsburgh win that took the air out of the Raiders.

Now, there is no love lost between the Raiders and 49ers, whether it be Oakland owner Al Davis or fans of both teams. Nevertheless, there is a natural tendency among sports fans to root for other local teams. A Raiders-49ers Super Bowl looked intriguing. In pro sports, it's a little different than college, where Cal and Stanford almost have a vested interest in each other's failure. Especially for kids, local pride and rooting interests are not burdened by old animosities. They just want the local guys to win.

HALL OF FAMERS

Jimmy Johnson was a five-time All-Pro cornerback who played his entire career with the 49ers. He started on offense and defense at UCLA. His brother was another famed Bruin, 1960 Olympic decathlon champion Rafer Johnson. Growing up in Kingsburg, a San Joaquin Valley town, Jimmy was saved from drowning by his "hero" Rafer as a child. He intercepted 47 passes and also played wide receiver early in his career. Johnson twice won the Len Eshmont Award for inspirational play and earned a Hall of Fame plaque in 1994.

That said, the 49ers faithful shrugged off the Immaculate Reception and got ready for the formidable threat of Roger Staubach and Dallas. The Cowboys under coach Tom Landry were almost a dynasty. In the 1960s they had lost two straight heartbreaking NFL title games to Vince Lombardi's Packers. Under the Texas good ol' boy Don Meredith and ex-California All-American Craig Morton, Dallas developed the reputation of a team that couldn't win the big one. This was a reputation that alternately hung around the necks of the Cowboys, the Raiders, the Vikings, the Rams, and the 49ers in the 1960s and 1970s.

Dallas had advanced to the 1971 Super Bowl on the strength of a 17–10 defensive struggle at San Francisco. That was not a good day for the bay: Oakland lost at Baltimore in the morning. After beating the 49ers, the Cowboys lost to Baltimore but shed their can't-win-the-big-one image the following season when ex-Navy Heisman hero Staubach finally took over as their quarterback for good.

In 1972, their first full season at the thoroughly modern Texas Stadium, Dallas found themselves in a dogfight with a team that had no business beating them, but managed to do it anyway. George Allen's Over the Hill Gang captured the NFC East. The intense Cowboys-Redskins rivalry hit full stride. Dallas made the playoffs as the wild-card but lost home-field advantage. The first round found them at Candlestick Park on a sunny afternoon.

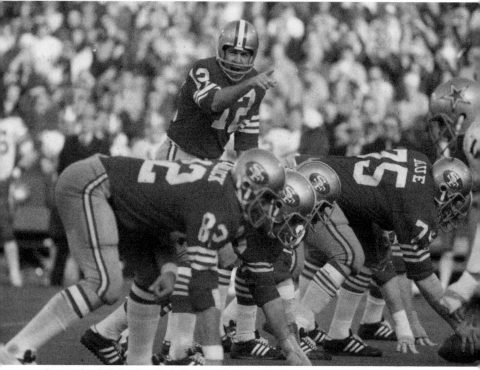

Quarterback John Brodie helped stake San Francisco to an early lead in its December 23, 1972, playoff game against Dallas, but Roger Staubach came off the bench and led the Cowboys to a come-from-behind 30–28 win over the 49ers.

San Francisco was a solid pro football franchise but a notch below the best. Throughout the 1960s, George Allen's Los Angeles Rams dominated them. The Rams of that era were one of the best teams never to win a Super Bowl. They were snakebit in freezing Minnesota or found some other excuse not to win, but the 49ers were just a bump on their winning road. When Allen left Los Angeles and took over in Washington, UCLA's Tommy Prothro became the coach of an aging team in L.A.

From 1970 to 1972, an odd conundrum shadowed the rivalry. After beating L.A. in 1970, the 49ers could not overcome the Rams at home or away. But the Rams fell over themselves against the rest of the league, allowing San Francisco to win three straight division crowns.

Coach Dick Nolan's squad was veteran, experienced, and injury-prone in 1972. Star quarterback John Brodie went down in the fifth game but was capably backed up by Florida Heisman Trophy winner Steve Spurrier. He kept the team in contention for nine games until Brodie's return, when the former Stanford signal-caller relieved Spurrier, engineered two touchdown drives, and beat Minnesota 20–17, clinching the West.

Nobody was confusing the Niners with the 1966 Green Bay Packers, but nobody else in the NFC resembled Lombardi's champions, either. The power had shifted to the American Football League, now the AFC, and with a few variations on the theme remained there ever since, with the exception of San Francisco's (and Dallas') dominance in the 1980s and early '90s.

Dallas, their first-round opponent, was in a state of confusion all day long. Behind Morton they had defeated San Francisco in the 1970 NFC title game. Staubach directed them to a 14–3 victory on January 2, 1972, en route to a Super Bowl victory over Miami. The '71 Cowboys are regarded as one of history's better teams, but success in Dallas leads to the kind of pagan idolatry that makes it hard to maintain the discipline that is necessary to win year after year.

It seems hard to believe in the retelling, since Staubach is a Hall of Famer, a winner, and a quarterback who gets more than a little support in the "he's better than Montana" argument, but he was inconsistent and *on the bench* while the Niners built a seemingly insurmountable lead.

Vic Washington returned the opening kickoff 97 years, and Brodie engineered two touchdown drives, good for a 21–13 halftime edge. The Candlestick crowd smelled blood. San Francisco looked fast, and Dallas looked confused—arguing amongst themselves, the taskmaster Landry threatening to "delete" them from his famed computer. It was the kind of home-field celebration that builds momentum until the snowball cannot be stopped. The radio and TV announcers all but declared victory for the 49ers and prognosticated the results of a 49ers-Redskins title bout, when Larry Schreiber scored his third TD, giving the home team a 28–13 lead entering the fourth quarter.

Dallas came out in the fourth quarter and turned it around immediately...not! Instead, they seemed to have given up. Consternation and recriminations were the order of their day. There was always something controversial brewing below the surface with these guys, a fact exemplified by books, novels, and movies that told tales out of school about them.

The clock kept ticking. Dallas foundered. The crowd celebrated. The 49ers congratulated themselves. The scribes wrote their game stories and worked their way toward the locker room. Victory was secure.

Staubach came off the bench. The man who had led his team to the Super Bowl a year before had been benched. It was back to the old quarterback question that had haunted Dallas as they transitioned from Meredith to Morton to Staubach...and now what?

Deep, *deep* down in the guts of only the most hardened, bitter, veteran fans were two sensibilities. One: San Francisco chokes. They had done it in 1957 against Detroit. In the world of pro football, there were ultimate champions and it was not them.

Two: Staubach already was a mythological figure of sorts. Those who had seen Montana weave his magic at Notre Dame could not shake the image of the '77 national title, the '78 'SC game, or the '79 Cotton Bowl from their minds as Joe delivered the goods at Candlestick. The same with "Roger the Dodger," who had beaten Notre Dame while at Navy. He had served as an officer and a gentleman. He was so upright, so clean. Could nice guys finish first?

DADDY DEAREST

Dick Nolan took over a moribund 49ers team in 1968. A Maryland alum, Nolan led San Francisco to their greatest success prior to the Bill Walsh era. He was in charge from 1968 to 1975, and helmed three consecutive Western Division champions (1970–1972). His son, Mike Nolan, grew up hanging around the 49ers practice field, and in 2005 was named coach of the team but was fired midway through the 2008 season.

That said, the notion was *ridiculous*. The 49ers, like the movie mogul in that year's best movie, *The Godfather*, had said they "could not afford to look *ridiculous!*" Staubach delivered no horses' heads, just touchdowns. Not with five minutes left. Not with two minutes left. An earlier Toni Fritsch field goal had "cut" the lead to 28–16. Whoop-de-do. Roger hit Billy Parks on a meaningless 20-yard scoring strike with 1:30 remaining.

Okay, Bay Area fans remembered the 1968 *Heidi* game, when the Raiders came out of nowhere to beat the Jets after the movie about a little Swiss girl took over East Coast TV screens, but this was *ridiculous*. Wasn't it?

PAIN AND SUFFERING

The Five Worst Day's in 49ers History
1. 1972 playoff loss to Dallas
2. 1957 playoff loss to Detroit
3. 31–0 loss to Chicago in 1961 that ended Red Hickey's "Shotgun"
4. 1991 playoff loss to the New York Giants
5. Gale Sayers' six-touchdown game in 1965

With the score 28–23, Dallas went for the inevitable onside kick. Every human being from San Jose to Santa Rosa and beyond knew it was coming. All the "good hands people" were there. So, it seemed, was God favoring His Chosen People, and they were not the guys playing for Baghdad by the Bay, as *Chronicle* columnist Herb Caen dubbed the place in the pre–Saddam Hussein era.

Dallas had it, and now Staubach looked like the Colossus of Rhodes. *Can he lead his team to a touchdown?* The Niners faithful watched like bystanders at a traffic accident. It had to be a TD, not a field goal. Suddenly, it was inevitable. The sensibilities of 60,000 people pleaded for San Francisco to hold on but knew they would not. They were right. Roger had a chisel and took a few well-placed stabs at his Hall of Fame plaque when he hit receiver Ron Sellers for the 10-yard touchdown pass that gave Dallas a 30–28 victory.

Few, if any, comebacks have been more improbable. Silence was broken only by the whoops of those Texans who made the trip, or who lived in the Bay Area like Al Qaeda sleepers. The Dallas players' shouts mixed with the *yee-haws*. The Candlestick denizens were too stunned even to boo. Eventually they moved, but they did not awaken for nine years. Brodie was ancient. The team was old. Everyone knew it was their last hurrah before the age of mediocrity that made up the remaining years of the decade, although few could have predicted the team would be quite as bad as they would actually be.

Salt would be added to the wound. Los Angeles became a dominant team again from 1973 to 1979.

THE O.J. SCANDAL

Orenthal James Simpson was not officially a member of the San Francisco 49ers when, on June 17, 1994, he and his pal, another San Francisco native and ex-49er named Al Cowlings, got in a white Bronco and apparently tried to make a Steve McQueen–style "escape to Mexico," as in the Sam Peckinpah film *The Getaway*.

He was also not officially a member of the USC Trojans or the Buffalo Bills. At the time, he was officially only a member of the Screen Actor's Guild and the Riviera Country Club. Official or not, however, all those organizations—USC, the 49ers, the Bills, not to mention the Potrero Hill Boy's Club, Galileo High School, and City College of San Francisco—jealously regarded him as a member in good standing of their respective "families."

O.J. of course "went Hollywood." He was a hero in New York. But he is San Francisco's, just as Joe DiMaggio belonged to the City despite Big Apple iconization and a Tinseltown marriage with Marilyn Monroe.

So when O.J. went down in flames, the City by the Bay looked inward and asked some hard questions. KNBR talkshow host Ralph Barbieri, a local guy predisposed to like O.J. and even to believe that a criminal had to be proven a criminal beyond all shadow of doubt before judgment is rendered, did not buy the Los Angeles jury's "not guilty" verdict for a second. He, like so many others, pronounced the man guilty in the court of public opinion.

That did not stop O.J. supporters from coming to his defense. One caller told Barbieri that he had to stop referring to him as "guilty" and "fallen," apparently not because of DNA or the weight of evidence against him, but because "O.J.'s from the neighborhood, man."

Barbieri was flabbergasted at that logic, but it is a pervasive argument that continues to percolate in the various "neighborhoods" that may resemble the one O.J. grew up in, but "escaped" from the first minute he had the chance.

The "neighborhood" of specificity is Potrero Hill, a gritty, mostly black section of public housing set in the hills overlooking Candlestick Park and the Hunter's Point–Bayview. The conundrum of this neighborhood is that it, like much of San Francisco, consists of spectacular vistas that might mean million-dollar homes in another city. In San Francisco, even the projects are aesthetically pleasing.

His mother raised O.J. His father mostly was not around. He often hung out around Candlestick, frequently enough to befriend the great Willie Mays, who followed his high school and junior college career with interest, declaring, "You have an unusual talent."

That talent came to fruition at City College of San Francisco. O.J. had attended Galileo High School, which is basically a middle class school located in the city's North Beach section. Historically, North Beach was home to Italian immigrants. DiMaggio grew up there and "attended" Galileo, although in truth he flunked out and started playing professionally for the San Francisco Seals at age 16.

CAN'T ANYBODY HERE PLAY THIS GAME?

Although recent 49ers teams in the Denise DeBartolo–John York era threatened, it is hard to say any team was worse than O.J.'s 1978 squad. They were 2–14. The hated Rams beat them twice. They started 0–4. Coach Pete McCulley was fired nine games into the season, replaced by Fred O'Connor. Eventually, O.J. was sidelined in favor of Paul Hofer.

O.J. normally would have gone to Balboa or Poly, but he was getting in a lot of trouble as a youth. He ran in a "gang," which by today's standards would be considered tame compared to the guns-and-drugs culture of the modern inner city. He was sent to Galileo High School in the hopes that the environment would straighten him out, and for the most part it did. His boyhood friend from the neighborhood, Al Cowlings, tagged along for the ride.

By the time O.J. entered Galileo, however, the Italian population was dispersing to the suburbs, mostly Marin County. The football teams O.J. played on consisted of a large number of Asian Americans. "Asians just aren't very big," O.J. wrote in his autobiography. "They didn't block much so I was on my own."

O.J. played defense. As a running back, he was not yet developed. As a student, he was lackluster despite a charismatic personality that made him the leader wherever he went. There were no college scholarships offered. O.J. considered joining the army, but his high school coach told him to get some education and use football to do it; that the army was just a form of social welfare and "you'll never get anywhere by having people give you things."

Whether the army-as-welfare analogy had merit or not, O.J. decided to give football, and education, another try. He enrolled at City College of San Francisco. CCSF was just another junior college, but O.J.'s two years there spurred the school into something very unusual.

BEST WINNING PERCENTAGE OF 49ERS COACHES

1. George Seifert, .755 (1989–1996)
2. Buck Shaw, .638 (1946–1954)
3. Bill Walsh, .618 (1979–1988)

San Francisco in the years since then has certainly not been a hotbed for prep sports. In the Bay Area, the players tend to come from the East Bay, San Jose, and the peninsula. The real focus of high school sports is in Southern California; Orange County, the San Fernando Valley, and the L.A. suburbs and inner city. Great juco sports programs have, over the years, emerged in the Southland, as untold numbers of great high school stars, not quite ready for prime time, hone their skills for a year or two before getting drafted in baseball or taking an athletic scholarship someplace. Despite little actual San Francisco talent to draw from, CCSF built on the O.J. legend to become without question the greatest junior college football tradition in American history. They draw from not only the entire Bay Area, but all over America, as well. Countless players from Texas, Florida, Ohio—some after leaving high-profile four-year programs after their freshman years—come to CCSF, drawn not only by the program's success but the chance to live in an interesting city.

As CCSF has developed into something beyond superlative, so too has another unlikely local program. De La Salle High School of Concord, located in the East Bay, won 151 straight games and is, like CCSF, the finest program in the nation at its level. The greatness of CCSF and De La Salle has had the effect of diminishing bragging rights in the Southland, where folks tend to think of themselves as a little bigger, a little better, a little brighter.

This state of affairs owes itself in no small part to O.J. His numbers at CCSF were staggering, almost cartoonish. After his freshman year, he was considered the biggest recruit in the nation, but his grades were still lagging. He had put in little effort in high school, little more as a college freshman.

Arizona State was willing to waive their requirements and let him into school, but no others were. Considering how many academic rejects play big-time collegiate sports, it is staggering to consider just how bad O.J.'s grades must have been up to that point, if nobody was willing to let this kind of superstar into its program.

Enter Marv Goux, the fiery assistant football coach at USC. Goux got wind of O.J.'s decision to enter Arizona State. He flew to San Francisco and counseled O.J. that "good things come to those who work for it." He said that if he would hang tough for one more year at City College, bring his grades up, and play another year of juco ball, then he would have the chance to achieve his dream of becoming a Trojan.

After nine years in Buffalo—including an amazing five-year stretch in which he amassed nearly 7,700 yards—Hall of Fame running back O.J. Simpson finished his career with two rather pedestrian seasons with the 49ers, 1978 and 1979.

O.J. was more than a man among boys his sophomore year at CCSF. He was a giant among pygmies. Indeed, he did transfer with a full scholarship to USC, and the rest, as they say, is history.

O.J. led Troy to the 1967 national championship and won the 1968 Heisman Trophy. An analysis of his 1967 season reveals that he should have won the Heisman that year, too, instead of UCLA's Gary Beban. His pal Cowlings followed him to USC. A talented lineman in his own right, Cowlings became a member of USC's famed "Wild Bunch" defensive front, named after the 1969 Sam Peckinpah movie.

In 1969 O.J. was the No. 1 choice in the NFL Draft, picked by the Buffalo Bills. He signed for a huge bonus and within a few years was the best player in the league. In 1973 he broke Jim

Brown's all-time single-season rushing record, becoming the first player to run for more than 2,000 yards. Others have done it since, but O.J. achieved the feat in a 14-game season. The league went to 16 games in the late 1970s.

At the height of his career, O.J. was not only the best player in the NFL, but had many people actively considering the possibility that he was better than Brown, the greatest pro football star in history. Injuries slowed O.J. down, and a review of his career reveals that as great as he was, he probably fell a little shy of Brown's greatness. Others have surpassed his records in the years since, but in his heyday he was something to behold.

O.J.'s career was made in little Buffalo, a small town in western New York that suffers from some of the worst weather in pro football. The California kid, who played in sunny Los Angeles as a collegian, achieved his bona fides playing in snow and sleet, which served only to add to the legend.

In an era of "Broadway Joe" Namath in New York, glamour teams in Los Angeles, Oakland, Miami, Pittsburgh, and Dallas, the biggest superstar of them all was O.J. Simpson.

O.J. left Buffalo in 1978 and came home to San Francisco. The Niners had floundered, but hope was held out that he was still a great runner who could lead the team he rooted for as a kid to glory. It was not to be. O.J. played two years at Candlestick Park (he was a teammate of Joe Montana's in 1979). His skills had deteriorated rapidly. He was a shadow of his old self. He was cheered on by the 49ers Faithful, but unable to produce on the field.

In 1979 Cowlings joined him on the 49ers. The O.J.-Cowlings friendship is very unique, in that they grew up in the same neighborhood and played Pop Warner, high school, junior college, college, and professional football together.

O.J. retired for a career in the movies. This was a natural transition that had started when he went to "Hollywood's school," USC. He acted in a number of films while still playing pro football, including *The Klansmen* and *Towering Inferno*. It is in examining the O.J. persona, his screen image, his personal charisma, where he is separated from other athletes; and where his eventual fall from grace is made so astounding.

He is a unique and iconic American personality. There had never been anything like him before he came along. He was *perfect!* First of all, O.J. was one good lookin' dude; his personality was charming, his allure and his appeal universal. His Hertz commercials, in which O.J. runs through an airport in a full suit, with a little old lady yelling, "Go, O.J., go!" is a classic in the advertising genre. But O.J. was highly intelligent, too. Not intelligent as in Ivy League intelligent; not a guy who was going to hold an audience in a discussion of the Middle East—"although I had been to Detroit a couple of times," as he joked on *Saturday Night Live*— but intelligent in the manner of friendly conversation, articulate, a smiling presence.

O.J. became an announcer, joining for a time the famed *Monday Night Football* crew of Howard Cosell and fellow USC alum Frank Gifford. His performances were never great, but his comic turn as the unfortunate Nordberg in the *Naked Gun* franchise is very funny stuff.

His friends, other than Cowlings and some old teammates, tended to be corporate sponsors, USC alums, the Hollywood crowd. O.J. became a golf addict, a constant presence at the exclusive Riviera Country Club in the posh Pacific Palisades–Brentwood enclave of L.A.

He had married his childhood sweetheart, Marguerite, bringing her with him to USC. At first, the "family man" act played well at 'SC, as if O.J.'s wife would "protect" him from all those beautiful coeds. O.J. started a family and went into the professional ranks, but fame, travel, money, and temptation were too great. He philandered, and the marriage ended in divorce. In 1977 O.J. went to a restaurant and flirted with a beautiful blonde girl from Orange County named Nicole Brown.

She was thrilled to get the attention of such a superstar and was encouraged to play this hand for all it was worth, which is what she did. She and O.J. were married. They had a family. They lived what seemed to be a perfect life in Brentwood. Nicole had money, a "rich and famous" lifestyle, trendy friends and clothes. O.J. lived a life most just dream of—golf, parties, fame, adoration...and any woman he wanted.

The marital infidelities caused problems, but like the couple in the Eagles song, O.J. and Nicole had checked in to the Hotel California, but they could never leave. An arrangement of sorts was entered into. There were rumors that Nicole played around as well. She became friendly with a number of O.J.'s handsome pals, fueling speculation further.

In 1989 O.J. became enraged about something and struck Nicole. She called 9-1-1 and told the operator that she was afraid Simpson would kill her. O.J. was arrested and given probation and some anger counseling. Nobody wanted to hurt the great O.J. It was "understood." He cheated on her, she cheated on him. Alcohol was involved. Drugs were involved. O.J. was a hero to millions, still had an acting career. The veneer was maintained.

The tabloids and psychologists have tried for years to get to what set O.J. off on June 12, 1994. He and Nicole were separated by then, but he was still a part of her life. She loved him and could not break from him completely. Despite having a *Playboy* party lifestyle, O.J. was tied to Nicole, and no other woman had a hold on him in that manner. The speculators, trying to figure it all out, said that O.J. was infuriated by Nicole's sexuality but was particularly appalled by her dating young, pretty men. No longer young, no longer the symbol of American sports heroism, O.J. seemed to be particularly frustrated by this dynamic.

Enter Ron Goldman. His role in the O.J. case is still a bit of a mystery to this day, but it appears that he was little more than an innocent victim, virtually a bystander who happened to be in the wrong place at the wrong time. Goldman was young and handsome, like so many a Hollywood wannabe working as a waiter in a trendy Brentwood bistro while waiting for his big break in the

A RAY OF HOPE

Steve DeBerg from San Jose State University was a competent NFL quarterback despite the record of 49ers teams he quarterbacked before Joe Montana took over. In 1979, under the tutelage of Bill Walsh, he broke Fran Tarkenton's NFL record for completions with 347.

THE PAC-10 CONNECTION

Frankie Albert was a Stanford All-American. Bill Walsh had two tenures at Stanford. Steve Mariucci coached at Cal. Terry Donahue coached at UCLA. The 49ers often looked to the Pacific-10 Conference for coaches and executives. After George Seifert stepped down, in the mid- to late 1990s the 49ers basically "stole" Mariucci from the California Golden Bears, where he had marginal success but was considered a hot coaching prospect. Mariucci coached good teams in San Francisco, continuing success with the team Walsh and Seifert had built. Walsh came back to the front office, eventually turning things over to Donahue. When it was all said and done, Walsh's absence coincided with the team's failures.

movies or modeling. On June 12, 1994, O.J. attended a dance recital at his daughter's school, but was not invited by Nicole to a dinner afterward. Goldman waited on Nicole and her party. He knew her from frequenting the restaurant. They flirted. Beyond that, nobody really knows.

Perhaps O.J. was infuriated at being cut out of the celebration of his daughter's dance recital. Perhaps the smiling, alluring Goldman capturing Nicole's attention was too much for him to take. Perhaps he had been planning it for weeks, for months. Perhaps, also, he did not commit the crime. Others have completely discounted this possibility, but the old saw "guilty beyond a shadow of a doubt" is a heavy burden on the state. The evidence against him is overwhelming, but in the interest of truth, justice, and fairness, there remains a scintilla of possibility that the crime was committed by another.

Scintilla: a bit, a tiny part, very little.

The facts in a nutshell are these: O.J. bought a knife at an L.A. knife store that was similar to the one used in the crime. He lived a few blocks away from Nicole, who stayed in their Brentwood home. Kato Kaelin, who lived in the guesthouse out back, heard a noise. Nicole had left her watch at the restaurant. Goldman found it and drove it to her house to return it. An assailant emerged and killed them with a knife. It was a gruesome double-murder.

If O.J. did it, he likely would have been hiding in the bushes. Whether he came to kill Nicole, and Goldman just happened to show up, or whether Goldman was more involved and therefore targeted by O.J., is not definitive.

O.J. was scheduled to fly to Chicago that night. A cab took him to the airport. The taxi driver said he was sweating profusely and appeared agitated. The next day the bodies were discovered. He was called and asked to return to L.A. The news hit the world like a bombshell.

The speculation immediately began to center on whether O.J. had done it. The LAPD considered him the prime suspect from the get-go. A few days after the murder, for reasons that neither O.J., Al Cowlings, nor anybody has ever adequately explained, Cowlings put O.J. in the back of a white Bronco and drove south, apparently with the intent of "escaping" to Mexico. The authorities got wind of it. Cell phone calls were made communicating with the car. It became public, and a bizarre slow speed chase on L.A.'s rush-hour freeways, which opened up like the Red Sea, played itself out for the world's cameras. It was as crazy a sight as many people have ever observed. Eventually, the car returned to Brentwood, where O.J. surrendered to authorities.

A trial was held. It was one of the most racially divisive events in modern American history, coming on the heels of the Rodney King beatings and 1991 L.A. riots. A downtown L.A. jury acquitted O.J. in 1995 to the consternation of millions. The verdict satisfied nobody.

More than a decade has past. O.J. was able to protect enough of his assets to live a golf course life in Florida, occasionally granting interviews in which he vowed to find "the real killers," and even emerging at sports shindigs to gladhand with the curious. To many young people, he is a strange figure, but to those old enough to recall his heyday, his story is utterly incredible. He was not merely a "big name" or a "star." He was *the* guy who had it all, a symbol of the new, better America. He was a universally loved figure with offers of a free lunch from coast to coast.

As mentioned, the evidence against him was overwhelming. It is the consensus of most that, had they sat on the jury that judged him, they would have found him guilty, but absent video evidence the smallest possibility resonates in a tiny segment of the population that somehow it was a drug deal gone bad, a mob retaliation, or some other explanation can be attached. The defense's assertions of a police frame based on racism have been discredited and carry no weight at this point with people capable of clear thinking. O.J.'s life as he knew it ended: movie stardom, hero status, athletic glory recalled at USC, Bills, and 49ers old-timers days. If O.J. is innocent, then he must live with the consequences of a monumental twist of fate. If he is guilty, then he must live with himself and God.

Then came perhaps the most bizarre episode of them all. Simpson tried to write a book called *If I Did It*, possibly a confession of sorts, but an outraged public prohibited its publication. Then, almost as if to punish himself, Simpson went to a Las Vegas hotel room to retrieve memorabilia he believed was rightfully his. He brought some losers along to help. Guns were involved. The caper went awry, and O.J. was arrested. His "friends" turned on him. He was convicted of a crime that, in any other case, would have resulted in a warning, or probation. But the world, including the Nevada prosecutors, was determined to give him the jail time for this crime he had not done for the 1994 murders. It is in a small cell in Nevada that O.J. sits and ponders.

SOMETHING TO SAVOR

DYNASTY

The San Francisco 49ers' dynasty lasted from 1981 to 1994, or until 1998, depending upon one's standards. With all due respect for great teams of the pre–Super Bowl era (Tim Mara's Giants, George Halas' Bears, Curly Lambeau's Packers, Johnny Unitas' Colts, Paul Brown's Browns) and dynasties of the modern game (Vince Lombardi's Packers, Tom Landry's Cowboys, Al Davis' Raiders, Chuck Noll's Steelers, Bill Belichick's Patriots), the 49ers' run is the longest, most sustained, and most successful in NFL history.

The run includes two Hall of Fame quarterbacks (Joe Montana and Steve Young) and three coaches (Bill Walsh, George Seifert, and Steve Mariucci). In addition to the five Super Bowl victories, the Mariucci-Young teams of the mid- to late 1990s were excellent, albeit not Super Bowl clubs. San Francisco survived transition, replacing legends with capable second acts. They found a winning formula that stood the test of time.

Of all the great teams and moments, one stands out. That was the 1990 Super Bowl victory over Denver. If San Francisco was an empire, this was Caesar returning to Rome parading the prisoners from Gaul.

The 1981 club was a surprise champion. Many argue that the 1984 club was better, but the victory over John Elway and Denver in Super Bowl XXIV was so enormous as to surpass all other glory.

San Francisco won three world championships under Bill Walsh (1981, 1984, 1988). The '88 title was a hard-earned one. The team teetered on the brink, survived a less-than-stellar regular season, got hot in the playoffs, and rallied to beat Cincinnati in the Super Bowl.

Walsh retired and was replaced by George Seifert from Polytechnic High School in San Francisco. Seifert's hiring and success sheds light on an odd fact, which is that Northern California is the "coaches capitol of America." The Bay Area is not to be confused with Orange County, Texas, or Florida when it comes to producing high school football talent (although few other geographic locations rank much higher in actuality). Perhaps it is the leafy affluence that produces academic success, and in football terms, winning strategic thought, but excellent coaches seem to spawn from the 415, the 510, the 408, the 925, and the 707.

Dick Vermeil (UCLA, Rams Super Bowl champs) hails from little old Calistoga. Pete Carroll (USC national champs) went to Redwood High in Marin County. Walsh is from the San Jose area and coached at Washington High in Fremont before a long career in college and the pros. Paul Hackett, one of the architects of the West Coast offense as a 49ers assistant, hails from Orinda. Bob Toledo, who had a good run at UCLA, is from San Jose and San Francisco State. John Madden (Raiders) and his boyhood pal John Robinson (USC, Rams) both came from Daly City. Walt Harris (Pittsburgh, Stanford) is from South San Francisco. Jack Del Rio of Hayward coaches the Jacksonville Jaguars. Mike Holmgren, like Seifert, went to Lincoln High and was considered a better prep quarterback than San Jose's Jim Plunkett before riding the bench

TAKE THIS GAME AND...

Also known as Riki Gray, Riki Ellison was "raised" in USC student housing by his single mother, who was pursuing her master's degree. Later a Trojans star, he became a starting linebacker for San Francisco from 1983 to 1988. After retirement, he became an expert on nuclear weaponry in the Washington, D.C., area.

at USC and coaching Green Bay to the Super Bowl title. With the exception of Del Rio (an 'SC All-American and Vikings star), none of these men were considered great players at the college or pro levels.

Seifert was a defensive expert, a guy with the perfect, quiet mind and demeanor to work with the more flamboyant, media-savvy Walsh. On a team of superstars, he was expected to maintain status quo, but he did more than that. Seifert is viewed by history as a guy who inherited greatness instead of developing it, but he deserves kudos because many coaches with talent find ingenious ways to screw it all up. He did not. The 1990 49ers indeed featured Holmgren as their offensive coordinator. Neither Holmgren nor Seifert "rocked the boat," so to speak.

"The team had been together for so long that roles were already defined," explained All-Pro linebacker Matt Millen (who came over after years of success with the Los Angeles Raiders), in *Super Bowl: The Game of Their Lives*. "The guy who stood tallest in the locker room was Ronnie Lott.... He was inherently a leader.... It drove him crazy when other defensive guys wouldn't play like he wanted them to play. He stuck to the defense, but I would say that Ronnie was the heart and soul of the entire 49ers team."

Millen referred to Montana as "Joe Cool." Lott was verbal. Montana was quiet, and in that quiet demeanor he led the team, giving them supreme confidence in themselves.

Wide receiver Jerry Rice, by 1990 established not only as the finest wide receiver in the NFL but already eliciting commentary that he might be the greatest *ever*, was "almost inhuman to me," said Millen. "I thought this guy was a freak of nature. No one could work like that and not be tired."

Rice had grown up learning how to catch actual bricks, thrown to him by his father, a mason. The opposite of Rice, both in terms of field position and personality, was the other talented receiver, John Taylor. Perhaps, had he possessed Rice's intensity, he would have been a Hall of Famer, too, but he certainly enjoyed some big moments with the 49ers.

Roger Craig out of Nebraska was a tremendous running back, complemented by the workmanlike Tom Rathman, who was willing to handle the role of blocker. Craig, like Rice, was literally a physical *specimen*, and he possessed focus as well.

Millen, despite a great reputation forged in L.A., knew that on this team he needed to earn respect. Normally a physical player in practice, he had to adjust to the 49ers' method, which did not focus on this type of approach, but in the games he, Lott, Charles Haley, and Michael Carter established their respective bona fides.

San Francisco operated a revised 3-4, but with Millen taking over the middle and calling signals, they became a 4-3. There was little situational substitution and not much blitzing. Their philosophy can be compared to John Wooden's man-to-man defensive approach during the heyday of UCLA basketball. With superior talent, they did not need to rely on tricks or surprises. The Niners operated out of a "man-zone" in which roles were specifically adhered to based upon a logical play progression. It was the kind of system that only works if the players have the size, speed, and ability to make it successful. Seifert was disciplined enough to let it operate in this manner, rather than push the proverbial "panic button."

Nineteen eighty-nine was arguably Montana's best year, and the 1989 49ers offense is considered by many to be the best "ever to grace the field in the National Football League," according to Millen. Their legend had been made on a *Monday Night Football* game at Anaheim when Joe directed the team to a remarkable comeback win over the Rams. Montana's statistics generally are not as impressive as some of the other great quarterbacks, namely Dan Marino and John Elway, to name a couple. He is considered a "winner" above all statistics, but in 1989 he put up impressive single-game and single-season numbers, carrying that into the postseason.

After a 14–2 regular-season mark, San Francisco opened the playoffs with Minnesota, who had humiliated them in 1987. Montana directed a total conquest of the Vikings, 41–13.

John Robinson's Rams were next. Perhaps they held out hope that the team that led San Francisco well into the second half before collapsing a month and a half earlier could maintain that kind of effort for four quarters. Instead, San Francisco dominated

No, he couldn't fly, but Joe Montana looked a lot like Superman during his January 28, 1990, performance in the 49ers' 55–10 pummeling of Denver in Super Bowl XXIV. Montana was named the MVP after throwing five TD passes in the game. Photo courtesy of AP Images.

from start to finish, 30–3. In many ways the game capped the changing dynamic of the San Francisco–Los Angeles sports landscape. Prior to Joe Montana, the Dodgers dominated the Giants, and the Rams had their way with the 49ers. This mirrored the North-South sociology, with L.A. considering themselves superior, San Francisco green with envy because of it. Now it was different.

Not only were the Rams a pale "rival" of the 49ers, but in 1989 both Bay Area baseball teams, the A's and Giants, made it to the World Series.

For Millen, it was his third Super Bowl, having made it to New Orleans in 1981 and again to Tampa in 1984, both with the Raiders. The 1990 Super Bowl was also in New Orleans; San Francisco's fourth in nine years. They needed to win it in order to match bragging rights of the 1974 through 1979 Steelers.

Millen had been on a Raiders team that, according to myth at least, had partied in New Orleans the week of their easy 27–10 win over Philadelphia in 1981. The 49ers were much more corporate in nature. Little in the way of hijinks was reported.

The AFC champions were the Denver Broncos, making their third Super Bowl appearance in four years with young quarterback John Elway, a hotshot from Stanford. Elway possessed all the tools Montana did not: size, speed, a rocket arm, and all-around athleticism. Going strictly by the book, there was no comparison. Elway was the better prospect. But of course every intangible favored Joe. That said, Elway was so good and had been so close for several years now, it seemed that his time had come. It was assumed that in order to defeat Denver, San Francisco would have to win an offensive shootout. But defensive coordinator Ray Rhodes, team leader Ronnie Lott, and Charles Haley made no such concessions.

Lott in particular had faced Elway when he was at USC. In his mind, Trojans dominance would carry over to 49ers dominance.

When the hoopla finally came to an end and the game started in front of 72,919 on January 28, 1990, at the New Orleans Super-dome, Elway was off and the Broncos were stopped stone cold. Montana responded by moving San Francisco down the field as if Denver was a high school team. It was 7–0 just like that. Whether Denver tried a zone or man-to-man, their defensive capabilities were no match for San Francisco, especially rested after the NFC title game—fully prepared, healthy, revved up.

TRIVIA

How many times was Randy Cross selected as All-Pro?

Find the answer on page 169.

NUMBERS DON'T LIE

1,502—Yards gained by Roger Craig in 1988, establishing a club record

Elway led the Broncos to a field goal to make it 7–3, which served only to stir up the 49ers' offense even more. A Broncos fumble was recovered by the Niners at midfield. Montana led them in for a score, hitting tight end Brent Jones on a short pass to make it 13–3.

In the first half, San Francisco used ball-control—utilizing Tom Rathman's running, blocking, and short-pass catching in combination with quick strikes. Jerry Rice broke free and scored on a Montana pass. At the half, it was all but over: 49ers 27, Broncos 3.

"We had to guard against getting excited, although we knew we were the world champs," said Millen.

Denver was a beaten crew and they had no chance of regaining respectability in the second half. That was when Montana & Co. separated themselves from the pack. Their victory goes down in history as the most impressive Super Bowl win ever. In comparing Lombardi's Packers, Don Shula's Dolphins, Chuck Noll's Steelers, and other contenders, none match what San Francisco did.

As the Niners turned the game into a track meet, frustration and defeat were etched on the Denver faces. In later years Elway said that the Denver coaches insisted that San Francisco would not throw in the middle, and prepared that way. Instead, Montana hit Rice and Taylor in the middle, attacking that area consistently.

"How could we be so dumb?" lamented Elway.

Rice caught three TD passes to set a record. Montana was the MVP of the game, a 55–10 trouncing. It was his third such award, added to his 1989 Player of the Year and Sportsman of the Year honors. At one point, Millen tackled Elway and consoled him by saying, "Hang in there, John."

In the aftermath of the Super Bowl, San Francisco had all the earmarks of being the finest pro football team ever assembled.

Their stars were all young and in their prime, with no great injury problems. They had tied the four–Super Bowl record of Pittsburgh and were immediately installed as favorites to repeat in 1990. A fifth Super Bowl win would cement their place in history. No team had ever won three in a row, although the 1965 through 1967 Packers were three-time NFL champions (the first of those coming before the Super Bowl).

It was the height of Montana's career. The 49ers could make a strong argument that they had the best quarterback (Montana), the best wide receiver (Rice), and the best defensive back (Lott) of all time. That argument holds to this day.

SUPER BOWL XIX: 49ERS 38, DOLPHINS 16

In 1983 the 49ers advanced to the playoffs against a tremendous Washington club, led by Joe Theismann. In a battle of Notre Dame greats, San Francisco rallied with three fourth-quarter touchdowns, but two questionable calls did them in late. A Redskins field goal sent Washington, not San Francisco, to the Super Bowl.

"That bitter loss could have motivated or crushed us," said Montana. "If we had wanted it to bring us down and affect our play in 1984, we could have let it. It would have been easy. But we didn't do that because we had guys like Ronnie Lott, who wouldn't allow us to think like that. Ronnie was extra motivated because he had been called for the second penalty before Mark Moseley's winning kick, so he was one of the guys who pushed the team to get back to the playoffs the next season."

Nineteen eighty-four remains a special year in 49ers history, though it can be argued that it was or was not their best season. Their 15–1 regular-season record was the best. Several subsequent teams were 14–2, but the 15–1 mark remains a record few teams have ever matched. Only the 1972 Miami Dolphins, 14–0 in the regular season and 17–0 after the Super Bowl, and the 2007 New England Patriots, 16–0 in the regular season but Super Bowl losers are better.

The 1984 49ers did not have the running game of later teams, when Roger Craig came into his own. They did not have Jerry Rice yet, and their victory over Miami in the Super Bowl was impressive,

Hall of Fame quarterback Dan Marino was stymied by San Francisco's defense in his only Super Bowl appearance, a 38–16 49ers victory. Marino threw for just one touchdown and gave up two interceptions during the January 20, 1985, title game. Photo courtesy of AP Images.

yet not as thorough as the 1990 whipping of Denver, or even the 1995 destruction of San Diego.

However, they defeated Dan Marino and a Dolphins team that looked almost unstoppable. If San Francisco were to prevail, it seemed, Montana & Co. would have to score at will in a shootout. Montana indeed did lead his team to an offensive explosion, but the defense bottled up Marino.

THE APPLE DOESN'T FALL FAR FROM THE TREE

Nineteen eighties–era 49ers backup quarterback Jeff Kemp is the son of former Buffalo Bills quarterback, New York congressman, and 1996 Republican vice presidential candidate Jack Kemp.

Perhaps what separates this year from others was the fact that ultimate victory came before a partisan Stanford Stadium crowd. This made it a unique game in all of NFL history.

One loss to Pittsburgh prevented an unbeaten season. San Francisco rolled to their last nine wins in a row. The New York Giants and the Chicago Bears were no match in home playoff wins, 21–10 and 23–0, respectively. A victory over Miami at Stanford would make them pro football's first 18-game winner.

It was a team of leaders: Lott, Montana, Randy Cross, but "everybody on that team knew his job without anybody saying anything to them," said Montana.

Bill Walsh used psychology on the 49ers, especially Montana, who despite his status was still a young man in 1984. Walsh rarely complimented Montana, leaving the understood message that his performance was what he was capable of, and so it was just his job. When Montana would suffer a slight injury or take the bench at the end of a big win, Walsh would tell his backup something like, "Great game." Montana at first was upset that he never got those small words of encouragement until he understood that he was expected to be great.

"Bill expected that high level of me all the time, so for him to say something like that to me, I had to do something that was way-out-of-the-ordinary great," said Montana.

Roger Craig was an immediate-impact second-year player from Nebraska in 1984. Wendell Tyler was a talented running back from UCLA, although he had a lifelong problem with fumbles. Dwight Clark, Russ Francis, and Freddie Solomon were excellent targets for Montana in the West Coast offense. This was still the heyday of Walsh's mastermind offensive schemes, still considered novel concepts. Later, when John Taylor and Rice came on and added extraordinary speed, their passing game spread the field, but the 1984 team still played ball control on the ground and in the air.

Some 49ers and members of the media claim in retrospect that nobody gave San Francisco any respect prior to the Miami game; as if Marino's team had it won already. This is not entirely true. The game was expected to be close, but nobody wrote off Joe Montana and the 49ers.

Marino's targets were Mark Duper and Mark Clayton, two fabulous pass-catchers. He had thrown for over 5,000 yards and 48 touchdowns.

An offensive line of Bubba Paris, John Ayers, Keith Fahnhorst, Randy Cross, and Fred Quillan protected Montana. The game started, and Montana had a 25-play script, a staple of the Walsh strategy, although there were divergences based on situations.

"There were very few games where we went past eight or nine—maybe 10—plays of the script," explained Montana.

"Stay on an even keel; don't let any one thing be any bigger than any other," Walsh told his team ahead of time. The familiar surroundings of Stanford Stadium also relaxed the coach and his team.

San Francisco was held on their first possession and punted. The defense of Lott, Hacksaw Reynolds, and Keena Turner squared off against Miami's no-huddle offense. They scored on their first two possessions, an Uwe von Schamann field goal from 37 yards out, and a short touchdown pass. In between, Montana led San Francisco downfield for a TD. After the Dolphins went ahead 10–7, the Niners felt they might have to score every time they had the ball, so they amped it up. And that was what they did. Montana hit Craig from eight yards out. Montana scored on a six-yard run. Craig carried it in from the 2. Now it was 28–10.

BY THE NUMBERS

3—The number of times in a row tackle Keith Fahnhorst was named All-Pro (1983, 1984, and 1985).

"You want to give us short yardage; we'll take short yardage," Montana explained.

When Miami began to drop their linebackers, Craig and Tyler pounded for gains. Montana also had the chance to make some yards scrambling.

Miami's Reggie Roby, the best punter in the NFL, had an off day, helping the Niners in the field position war. Leading 28–10 was nerve-racking "because Danny was so dangerous—and I mean *really* dangerous," said Montana.

But Lott, Eric Wright, and Jeff Fuller stepped up big time. Still, two Miami field goals narrowed the halftime score to 28–16, and it wasn't over. But San Francisco scored on a Ray Wersching field goal and a Roger Craig slant to make it 38–16, and that's how it ended up. Miami coach Don Shula said his team suffered a "total breakdown."

"As soon as it's over, it's like, 'Oh, god, now what do we do?'" said Montana, which explains the conundrum of sports greatness, or political victory, or life in general: always another hill to climb. The 49ers would have a letdown and not repeat the trick for four more years.

"I know one thing I'll always remember fondly about Super Bowl XIX is that we didn't go away to play it," recalled Montana. "It's always nice to go some other place to play a Super Bowl because it is something special, but I don't think I would have preferred going away. It felt good to stay home, despite the many distractions. It gave us an opportunity to play in front of the home crowd and for the people of the Bay Area to see us win one Super Bowl in person."

CELEBRITY CORNER

Has anybody ever seen actor Tom Selleck and 49ers tight end Russ Francis (1982–1987) in the same room? Francis greatly resembled the popular *Magnum P.I.* actor, an athlete in his own right at USC. Francis is a native of Hawaii, where *Magnum* was so famously filmed.

A famous photo shows Walsh, carried on the backs of his team, the rim of the familiar Stanford Stadium in the gloaming background, the sun having set in the west. It does not get any better than that.

MAESTRO

Okay, here we go again. The age-old argument, "Who is the best ever?" George Washington or Abraham Lincoln? George Patton or Omar Bradley? Jascha Heifetz or Arthur Rubinstein? Giacomo Puccini or Plácido Domingo?

With the 49ers, there are many contenders. Greatest team ever? Hey, the 1984 49ers are happy to throw their hats in the ring with the '85 Bears and the '72 Dolphins. Best dynasty? Well, San Francisco in the 1980s will state its case against Lombardi's Packers or Chuck Noll's Steelers.

How about best quarterback? Sure, Montana is considered the best, but you will get plenty of support from fans of Roger Staubach or Johnny Unitas, or even old-timers who saw Sammy Baugh. Best coach? Well, there is Walsh, but there is also Lombardi, Paul Brown, Don Shula, Tom Landry...

Ronnie Lott? Probably the finest defensive back, but Deion Sanders, briefly a 49er, handled the position with as much aplomb, albeit in a totally different style. Then there is the wide receiver position. And now we really do not have much to argue about, because whether we are talking about style points or statistics, Jerry Rice stands head and shoulders above the competition. The other guys' place in history is not nearly as cut-and-dried.

Sure, you have your Don Hutsons, your Raymond Berrys, your Fred Biletnikoffs, your Paul Warfields, and your Lynn Swanns, but Rice is above all of them. San Francisco won two Super Bowls before he arrived, but captured three once he got there. Montana hooked up with him, but Rice allowed for a seamless transition to Steve Young.

Rice "redefined his craft," wrote *Sports Illustrated*'s Michael Silver. He caught more passes for more yards and more touchdowns than any player who ever lived. He earned Super Bowl and NFL Most Valuable Player awards.

In his three Super Bowl victories (over Cincinnati in 1989, Denver in 1990, and San Diego in 1995), Rice was at his best: 9.3 catches, 170.7 yards, and 2.3 touchdowns per game. At 6'2", 200 pounds, Rice did not have the height or overwhelming strength of modern big pass-catchers like Keyshawn Johnson or Terrell Owens. But Rice's work ethic was legendary. His body was so powerful that he withstood injuries and pain, fended off tacklers, and separated himself from the field time and time again.

TOP 10 GREATEST FOOTBALL PLAYERS OF ALL TIME

1. Jim Brown
2. Jerry Rice
3. Walter Payton
4. Joe Montana
5. Ronnie Lott
6. Lawrence Taylor
7. Johnny Unitas
8. Dick Butkus
9. Roger Staubach
10. O.J. Simpson

Rice's background was much different from his teammates and coaches. Montana and Lott were superstars at high-profile colleges, as was running back Roger Craig from Nebraska. Steve Young grew up in a bastion of wealth: Greenwich, Connecticut. Bill Walsh and George Seifert were middle-class Bay Area guys.

Rice, on the other hand, is a product of the Mississippi Delta. He saw sports as an escape, and vowed that when he made it, he would buy his parents a new house.

"Growing up in a small town taught me the meaning of doing the right things," he said. "Because the town was so small, if you did something wrong, it was gonna get back to your parents. And with my parents, that meant you would be disciplined, so I think it made me into a better person. There was a lot of bad stuff going around—kids stealing cars, doing drugs—but I feel that my parents raised me the right way. We didn't have all the money, we didn't have all the luxuries, but I think because we were so close it made up for all that. I think my upbringing molded me into the person I am today."

Rice played small town high school football, his skills not noticed by any major college powerhouse. But Mississippi Valley

State coach Archie "Gunslinger" Cooley recruited and landed him.

"No one else came to see me in person," said Rice.

Cooley ran one of the most pass-happy offenses in college football. Rice caught notice and then some. Mississippi Valley State put up outrageous numbers, and Rice's were the most outrageous. Before he was the greatest pro receiver ever, he may well have been the greatest college receiver ever. But playing at a small school, he was virtually unnoticed.

ESPN was barely a blip on the screen in those days. Bill Walsh was in a hotel room in Houston the night before a 1984 game with the Oilers. Just before turning the TV off and drifting off to sleep, Walsh heard the local announcer say, "We've got some highlights you won't believe coming after this."

Walsh kept his eyes open long enough to see something *he could not believe*. Rice scored five touchdowns, but Walsh immediately thought to himself that a player like that would never be available when his team drafted. The Niners were in first place and on their way to a Super Bowl title, meaning that unless they traded up, every team in pro football would draft ahead of them.

"I didn't know how it could ever be done," said Walsh, "but I had a fixation on Jerry from the time I watched those highlights."

Walsh decided he had to have Rice. There was none of the supposed "question" revolving around whether to draft Steve Dils or Joe Montana, Kenny Easley or Ronnie Lott.

Despite Rice's low-key college profile, his talent was well-known by the scouts come draft day. Walsh did trade up for New England's pick (No. 16). Kansas City passed on Rice with the 15th choice, and Jerry was a 49er.

Rice was "in awe" of Montana, who was at the height of his game in 1985. His first year, he had trouble holding onto the ball. In 1986 Rice was named the NFL's Player of the Year, but fumbled early in a playoff loss to the Giants. In 1987 Rice set an NFL record with 22 touchdown catches.

In 1988 the 49ers struggled to make the playoffs. Then the legend was made. He caught three first-half TD passes to lead San Francisco to a 34–9 victory over Minnesota. At Chicago, Rice came out in freezing pregame weather *sans* long sleeves, in an effort to psych the Bears. In reality, he almost psyched himself. "I was thinking, *I don't care, I can do whatever I want to out here today*," he said. "So I ran out there in my short sleeves, and I almost froze to death. I ran back into the locker room and put on long sleeves."

Montana and Rice put on a pass-catch display, crushing the Bears 28–3. Against Cincinnati in the Super Bowl, played at Joe Robbie Stadium in warm Miami, Florida, Rice caught 11 passes from Montana for 215 yards and a touchdown. The winning touchdown catch in the 20–16 victory, by John Taylor, can be attributed to Rice. Taylor was open because the Bengals concentrated everything they had on Rice.

"The second we took the field for the final drive, I knew we had the game won," said Rice.

Rice was named the game's Most Valuable Player.

Rice never got the endorsements of some of his heralded teammates, implying racism. The fact that Ronnie Lott was as loved as Montana destroyed that notion. Rice's problem was that, as a smalltown guy, he never became comfortable with the press. He was never a good interview, although he was always polite. Lott, a product of the media machine at USC, who carried himself like a guy running a self-help seminar, was a media darling. Montana could do no wrong—handsome, blond, beautiful wife, boy-next-door smile.

In 1989 San Francisco went 14–2 and came charging into the Super Bowl with Denver. Rice's early crossing-pattern catch-and-run for a 20-yard touchdown set the pace in the 55–10 destruction of the Broncos. Rice caught seven passes for 148 yards with three touchdowns.

In 1990 he became the fourth player to catch 100 passes in an NFL season, as the Niners cruised to another 14–2 record before getting upset at home in the NFC title game by the Giants. Montana was the league MVP, but Rice was named *Sports Illustrated*'s Player of the Year.

On October 29, 1995, Rice broke James Lofton's career record of 14,004 receiving yards. In 1995 he set the all-time record for yards

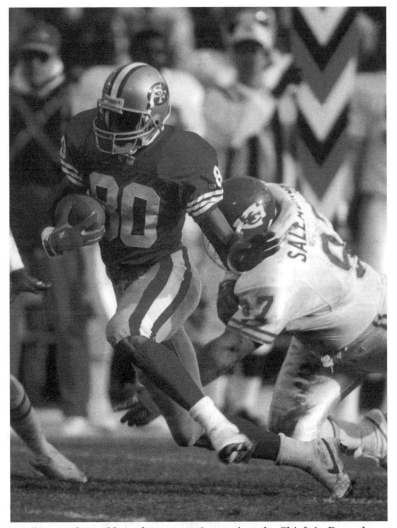

Jerry Rice evades tacklers after a reception against the Chiefs in December 1991. Was he the best receiver ever? Rice's No. 1 rankings in career receptions, yards, and receiving touchdowns offer strong evidence that he deserves the accolade.

in a season when he gained his 1,848th yard on December 24 at Atlanta. In that game he also broke Art Monk's career receptions record when he caught his 941st pass. He also broke Jim Brown's old record for career TDs of 126 when he ran for a score on a

NUMBERS DON'T LIE

22—Jerry Rice's team record for receiving touchdowns in a season (1987).

reverse on *Monday Night Football* against the Raiders in 1994. That year he was the winner of the Mackey Award.

"I can't think of another player that more exemplifies the drive, work habits, and commitment it takes to reach the top," said former 49ers assistant Mike Holmgren.

After the 49ers lost to Dallas, sending the Cowboys to their second straight Super Bowl in January of 1994, Rice's competitive nature was revealed when he expressed dismay at his teammate's casual attitude on the plane back to California.

The next year, he and quarterback Steve Young teamed up to lead San Francisco back to where they once belonged. Deion Sanders came over to shore up the defense. Coach George Seifert asked Rice whether he would "approve" of the flamboyant Sanders. The team leader by now, Rice just wanted to win. Sanders helped them achieve that end.

"He is so driven to be the best, and what I love about him is, once it became clear he was the best, he changed," said Young. "Instead of putting on a false 'I'm not the best' persona, he accepted it and redirected the challenge. He carries himself like he's the best ever; he's not afraid to do that. He's very comfortable with just being Jerry Rice."

In Super Bowl XXIX, the 49ers returned to Joe Robbie Stadium, site of their 1989 win over the Bengals. Young hit Rice for a touchdown on the game's third play from scrimmage. Their stunning 49–26 win over Junior Seau and San Diego was almost as impressive as their smashing defeat of Denver in the 1990 Super Bowl.

Toward the end of his time in San Francisco, Rice had to share the stage with Terrell Owens. Eventually, Rice went to the Oakland Raiders while the Niners put all their eggs in T.O.'s basket. Physically, T.O. was what Rice was not—bigger, stronger, more physical. Rice was the consummate professional, a man of class, a winner.

YOUNG MAN

Through the travail of ages, or at least in the 20th and 21st centuries, professional athletes have often been less-than-stellar characters. In the 1900s fathers did not let their daughters date ballplayers. Fancy hotels turned them away. Then a collegiate, All-American type, baseball star Christy Mathewson, changed the perception of the athlete.

Mathewson seemed to be an exception. Fans have often found athletes to be spoiled, overpaid, uninformed, undereducated, and self-indulgent. In San Francisco, the poster boy for each of these adjectives has been the one and only Barry Bonds.

Sometimes, very rarely, an athlete comes along who is that rarest of entities: a great star on the field, a role model human being, handsome to a fault, who possesses the education and intellect of a college professor. Thus: Steve Young.

Steve Young was the Jack Armstrong of his era. There is a sense that Young could do whatever he chose to do. If he decided to enter politics, he likely would be successful. (Young has supported Republicans, but there is no indication that he ever plans to throw his hat in the ring.)

He grew up in an upper middle-class family. His father was an attorney. The family moved from Mormon Utah to one of America's wealthiest enclaves, Greenwich, Connecticut. Greenwich is not considered a bastion of high school sports, and for this reason, perhaps, Young was not as heralded as he might have been.

His religious background directed him to Brigham Young University, at a time in which the Cougars were the most explosive passing team in the land. Before Young, Gifford Nielsen and Jim McMahon lit up the collegiate football world. Young was arguably the best of them all, but not the last. Marc Wilson, Robbie Bosco, and Ty Detmer followed in his footsteps.

It was tough for Young at first, and as a freshman he was eighth on the depth chart. But the coaching staff fixated early on the 6'2", 215-pound southpaw as McMahon's heir apparent. When McMahon departed for pro success, Young took over and shined. After an All-American career in which he added to the numerous Cougars passing records, Young made the decision to go with the fledgling U.S. Football League. The USFL had signed Herschel Walker of Georgia and looked to be a success.

Young hooked on with the Los Angeles Express. It was a bittersweet experience. He was made instantly wealthy, as the league had money to spend on young stars. He also was given instant freedom to run a wide-open, BYU-style offense that featured his multiple talents as a passer, scrambler, and pure runner. Looking back, his wild running could easily have resulted in a career-threatening injury, but he was lucky. Those who saw him with the Express were amazed at his talents. He was nothing less than remarkable, but the problem was that the people who saw him were few and far between.

The Express toiled in the mammoth Los Angeles Memorial Coliseum, which made their sparse crowds look even more embarrassing. The L.A. media gave them scant attention, TV ratings were poor, and the league folded.

He then signed with the Tampa Bay Buccaneers, where he continued to display great ability in the mid-1980s. The Bucs were an also-ran. Playing for them garnered little attention.

In 1987 Bill Walsh surveyed the landscape—his own team and the league's—then made a visionary move, albeit one fraught with controversy. Up through the 1986 season, Joe Montana had won two Super Bowls and established himself as a superstar—the quarterback some were saying might be the best of all time. But as great as he was, there were question marks. Montana had experienced periodic, chronic back troubles. Not a big man—certainly not a hunk like Young—he appeared vulnerable on the field. He was an eight-year veteran entering 1987, and in the world of pro football, eight years is a long time. He had been the starter almost that entire time, meaning he had endured plenty of wear and tear. The team played in the postseason almost every year, so he was subjecting himself to more pounding than most other QBs.

Looking back with the benefit of hindsight, it seems incongruous, but in the mid-1980s there were rumors about Montana revolving around the question, "What's wrong with Joe?" So great was Montana in guiding the team to ultimate victory in 1981 and 1984 that his failure to do so in other years seemed to many fans a symptom not of a superior Redskins or Bears team, but of a failure, perhaps even a moral failing, on Montana's part.

The 1980s were a time of drug scandals in sports. Rumors of cocaine use revolved around Montana. Wild stories of Montana, passed out in hotel rooms, being revived by the team doctor just in time to go out and win a big game, began to circulate. Looking back, there is no viable reason to believe any of them, but Montana was such a celebrity above and beyond football that his life had reached tabloid level.

Walsh understood the timeline of NFL quarterbacks. Some have criticized him for doubting Montana, but he was looking to create a viable contingency, knowing that if the 49ers were to continue their great run beyond Montana's effectiveness at the position, a worthy successor must be chosen.

The Packers had nobody behind Bart Starr. The Dolphins had failed to adequately replace Bob Griese. The Steelers had no true replacement for Terry Bradshaw. Danny White was good in Dallas, but he was no Roger Staubach. Walsh was not about to change the essential nature of the 49ers to a team relying on defense or ball control. He had won with the West Coast offense, and if he was to continue to win, it would be with the West Coast offense. Beyond Montana, who had the smarts and the ability to make his complicated schemes work? He arranged to trade two draft picks to Tampa Bay for the man he felt could do just that: Steve Young.

Even though it was officially a trade, Young had leverage and could have arranged to go to another team. He chose San

INJURY FRONT

Steve Young suffered numerous concussions in the late 1990s, leading to a national debate over whether he should retire from the game (similar to what Troy Aikman went through in Dallas). Bill Walsh called him "the greatest player of the decade" in the 1990s. He called it quits after the 1999 season, and the team has never approached their old glory.

Francisco as much as they chose him. He must have felt Montana's time was limited and wanted to play for a winner, to thrive under the great Walsh, and to make his name once and for all.

Montana was nervous about Young for obvious reasons, even though Walsh told the media, "We fully expect Joe to continue as the leader and mainstay of our team."

Walsh had a tough balancing act, assuring Montana but privately telling Young that he would be the starter "in three years." At first, Young felt that the time would be good for him. He would learn from the best—Montana and Walsh—without great pressure. But in the 1987 and 1988 regular seasons, Montana had periods of inconsistency with nagging injuries. Young was brought in and performed brilliantly. His personal competitiveness became too much to bear.

"He was just frustrated," said former tight end John Frank, who roomed with Young in Los Gatos. "He was miserable. He couldn't stand it. I liked him because he was pretty clean cut. It was a lot of clean living, and I respected that and liked that. But he was very overbearing to live with sometimes because he wasn't playing."

Walsh's three-year timetable looked to be an insurmountable obstacle for Young. If it were to be adhered to, that would mean Young would be the starter by the 1990 season. In the first two years, he replaced Montana on occasion, sometimes because of injury, sometimes because of Joe's ineffectiveness. Young's obvious abilities were made apparent to teammates, coaches, media, and fans alike. Divisions were created.

Young and Montana are both affable personalities, naturally predisposed to liking each other, but the rivalry caused heated feelings. The rumors about Montana's drug use may or may not have affected the relationship, but Young was seen as a clean-living "Christian stud," not unlike the Hartman character who the hard-drinking Mac Davis character must fend off in the outrageous football flick *North Dallas Forty*.

Young had to deal with mixed emotions in 1988 and 1989. On the one hand, he sat on the bench, seeing his prime years drift by. On the other hand, he earned two Super Bowl championship rings on teams in which Joe Montana elevated himself from great to absolute legend.

Young might have expected that Walsh's promise that he would be the starter by 1990 would be kept, but it was an impossibility. His frustration came half out of a sense that he had been betrayed, half out of the fact that he knew in his heart Montana was the best in the game and nobody was going to bench him no matter how good he was. Young began to fear that he would never have the chance to prove himself.

By 1990 Montana had removed all doubt. His 1989 season goes down in history as the best ever, or close to it. His performance against Denver in the Super Bowl may be unmatched. In the 1990 regular season he provided more of the same, some might say better than before.

Young had no allies, not among teammates, coaches, fans, or media. His was a difficult situation. A trade would result in playing time, but likely with a non-contender, certainly not a champion of the 49ers level. He was still the heir apparent—if he could just wait it out, he would take over a team that could win Super Bowls. He could throw to Jerry Rice.

His biggest backer, Walsh, was gone. Retired after the 1988 season, he was now a college football TV analyst. Seifert was in, and he had not made any three-year promises to Young. Young was like the real-life movie character Rudy, who had been promised by Ara Parseghian he would dress for a game his senior year at Notre Dame, only to have the coach retire, replaced by Dan Devine, who had no obligations weighing on him.

The opening did not occur until the January 1991 playoff loss to the New York Giants. Montana injured himself. A fumble and missed opportunities gave victory to New York. Recriminations followed. Had San Francisco held the lead, they likely would have dispatched Buffalo in the Super Bowl, entering the 1991 campaign with three straight Super Bowl wins. There would have been no existing will to replace Montana.

Seifert made the decision that Young, the younger man, the future of the team, had to be given his shot in 1991. That decision, understandably, resulted in much consternation.

Steve Young searches for an open receiver during San Francisco's January 9, 1988, playoff loss to the Vikings. Young was still a backup to Joe Montana at this point, but he eventually took over the team and established himself as one of the greatest quarterbacks in NFL history.

Officially, Young led the NFC in passing efficiency in 1991, but such stats did not always result in victories. He suffered injuries himself, as did Montana. Steve Bono played well as a replacement for both of them. The team did not make the playoffs, with a preponderance of the blame landing on Young.

Montana didn't help the situation. The rivalry, from his standpoint, became a blood feud. Young maintained a diplomatic position, but Montana openly disliked, some say even hated, Young. He reacted with icy silence to Young, backstabbing him, talking behind his back, fomenting team divisions, lobbying the coaches and media.

Oddly, throughout his career, Montana's best friends on the team had been his backups, none of whom had ever been a threat. They were all decent second-string guys who knew their place and were honored just to carry Joe's water.

"Steve is on a big push for himself," Montana told the *Washington Post*. "Any time you have a competition, there is a certain amount of animosity. I can say we have only a working relationship. That's all it is. He's on my team, but as far as I'm concerned, he's part of the opposition. He wants what I have."

"In 1991 Joe wasn't very helpful," said Young. "But there was a transition time. People weren't sure what they were supposed to say, how they were supposed to react. Joe's very competitive, and I don't know any other way to be. We do very well considering we're very competitive. People think there are fistfights in the back room. That's not the case at all."

In 1992 Montana was recovered from his injury but lost the starting job forever to Young. He sulked, gave Young the silent treatment, and told anybody who would listen that a team he had turned from an also-ran into a juggernaut had betrayed him.

Young played brilliantly, establishing himself along with Dallas' Troy Aikman as the premier quarterback in the game. San Francisco went 14–2. The better Young performed, the pettier Montana appeared.

"Can this really be Joe Cool?" wrote C.W. Nevius in the *San Francisco Chronicle*. "The guy who stood in there until fire-breathing blitzing linebackers were inches from his chest and then sailed a perfect spiral into the end zone? We kind of picture you as Clint Eastwood. Lately you are starting to sound like Don Knotts."

Despite success on the field, the pressures got to Young. He had gone to BYU Law School over the previous off-seasons and seriously considered retirement in favor of a quiet legal practice. Teammates were cool to him. He had not yet taken them to the Promised Land. Joe was still their Moses.

"I think there was so much going on at that time that was really overwhelming," said Paulshe Adcock, a close friend. "He was trying to deal with it little by little. There were a lot of great expectations from other people, and he was trying to step in and

TRADING PLACES

Hall of Fame quarterback Steve Young was acquired from Tampa Bay in 1987 for that year's second- and fourth-round draft picks.

fill somebody's shoes that nobody wanted filled. I think he did the best he could do, considering everything."

As the 1992 season played out, Young's performance began to overcome the sentiment favoring Montana. Young won the league MVP award. If the team could win the Super Bowl, Young would be a hero. Washington fell in round one of the playoffs 20–13, and into town rode the upstart Cowboys.

Coach Jimmy Johnson had come over from the University of Miami, drafting Troy Aikman No. 1 out of UCLA. From the ashes of a 1–15 team in 1989 Johnson had built a champion. Aikman-to–Michael Irvin was now an aerial combo to equal the Montana-to-Rice or Young-to-Rice 49ers attack.

The 49ers were favored, and Young was excellent, completing 25-of-35 passes for 313 yards and a touchdown, but Aikman made his legend that day, going 24-of-34 for 322 yards and two touchdowns. Several penalties killed the 49ers, and Dallas prevailed 30–20. They defeated Buffalo in the Super Bowl to take the Brass Ring.

Young's agent, Leigh Steinberg, suggested that in light of the vociferous attacks made by the 49ers faithful against Young, he should look for another team, but Young was determined to win out in the City. Sportstalk radio had a field day:

"Joe would have seen [Ken] Norton."

"Joe wouldn't let himself get sacked by Charles Haley."

A letter to the *Chronicle* was signed from "Mormons for Montana."

Montana was finally let go in 1993. He took over as quarterback of the Kansas City Chiefs. He teamed with Marcus Allen, the great Raiders running back who had been forced out of Los Angeles by Bo Jackson, just as Montana had lost out to Young. The Chiefs returned to respectability, and Montana was able to finish his career, not in San Francisco, but at least on his own terms. After retirement, he was given a fabulous day at Justin Herman Plaza, and his relationship with the team was healed.

In 1993 many watched Montana in Kansas City and found further reason to despise Young. The Niners went 10–6, beat the New York Giants in the first playoff game, but found themselves in Dallas playing for the Super Bowl. It was not even close. Aikman separated himself from the rest of pro football's quarterbacks, beating Young and the 49ers 38–21, on their way to a second straight Super Bowl title.

In 1994 San Francisco traveled to Kansas City for Game 2 of the season. In a head-to-head matchup, Montana bested Young 24–17. From there, Young and his team came together. A key victory was a 21–14 win over Dallas, giving San Francisco home-field advantage in the playoffs.

The 13–3 49ers dispatched Chicago, then beat Dallas again, 38–28, to earn a trip back to the Super Bowl.

"It's your year," Aikman told Young at midfield after the game.

The crowd was *finally* with him, chanting, "Steve! Steve! Steve!" and then, "MVP! MVP! MVP!"

Young was off the charts in San Francisco's blowout 49–26 win over San Diego in Super Bowl XXIX in Miami.

"I wouldn't have believed it if I wrote it down," Young said after winning the game's MVP award. "Six touchdowns, it's impossible. I've played football for 25 years, and four is the most I ever threw."

Steve Young had arrived. From 1991 to 1994, Young was arguably, statistically during regular-season play, the greatest quarterback ever for a similar period. In the following years, he continued to play at the highest of levels. Brett Favre of Green Bay joined Young and Aikman among the game's elite QBs. The Packers defeated San Francisco in the NFC Divisional Playoffs in January 1996 and 1997. Young led his team to 11–5, 12–4, 13–3, and 12–4 records between 1995 and 1998, but no Super Bowls followed those seasons. Favre and Green Bay, John Elway and Denver, Kurt Warner and St. Louis tasted the fruits of victory.

Young suffered various concussions in the late 1990s, eventually forcing his retirement, and with that came the end of the 49ers' dynasty. It has never returned. The fact that he sat behind Montana from 1987 to 1990 may well have allowed him to save his body, playing a long career in pro football that resulted in his induction into the Hall of Fame.

Today Young is as associated with the team as Montana, in that he is a regular on KNBR, makes commercials, and is accessible to the media in general. He is a happily married family man. Young is an incredibly engaging, intelligent athlete—a true rarity in the sports world. He often pondered whether playing quarterback was a legitimate occupation when it came to serving his fellow man. A Super Bowl champion, a Hall of Famer, Young reached the highest of heights, yet to this very day there are still many who resent him because he replaced Joe Montana.

Montana lives in the Napa Valley, but there are no reports that the Youngs and Montanas take family vacations together.

WHEN THE FAT LADY SINGS

1957 VS. DETROIT

The Cleveland Browns of coach Paul Brown were a dominant force in the National Football League of the 1950s. The New York Giants' defense was legendary. Johnny Unitas turned Baltimore into a champion. These were the decisive powers of pro football in this uniquely American decade.

But in 1957 the Detroit Lions and San Francisco 49ers made it to the NFL playoffs. It was an opportunity for San Francisco to move into the upper echelon of the league, to earn respect. Mainly, when it was over, they earned for their efforts a certain amount of derision. Greatness in the league would have to wait.

Football, San Francisco, and America were still innocent compared with the decade that would come. Nineteen fifty-seven was the last year before the Dodgers and Giants came west. A recruiting scandal had recently rocked the Pacific Coast Conference—so much so that the University of California decided to downgrade the importance of football. They have never completely recovered from that decision.

The Pacific Coast League was still a "major" league, featuring great rivalries between the San Francisco Seals, Mission Reds, Oakland Oaks, Los Angeles Angels, Hollywood Stars, Sacramento Solons, San Diego Padres, and Portland Beavers.

Dwight Eisenhower was in the White House. The effects of McCarthyism dominated the body politic. The battle against

Communism was a worldwide struggle between good and evil, God and atheism—all set against a background of hydrogen bombs and the space race. Americans, at least most white Americans, lived the good life. Cars, freeways, refrigerators, air-conditioning, modern appliances, and numerous amenities fueled a suburbanized baby-boomer generation. World War II had been won. The United States was the greatest, most all-conquering power since Caesar's Roman Empire. Hubris filled the air.

The citizenry was sports-crazy. The rivalry between the Rams and 49ers reached a fever pitch. Crowds of well over 100,000 saw the two teams do battle when they played at the Los Angeles Memorial Coliseum. Horace Stoneham, owner of the New York Giants baseball team, saw the enthusiasm of San Franciscans for football and correctly judged that they would go for baseball in a like manner.

This was before Vietnam, before the free-speech movement at Berkeley, before antiwar protests in the streets. Drugs, free love, and radicalism were far-off concepts, even though they were in their strongest ascendancy via the beatnik presence, embodied by Jack Kerouac's *On the Road* and Allen Ginsberg's *Howl*, expressed right there in the cafes of San Francisco's North Beach. But it was still an *American Graffiti* age—the last really good decade in city prep sports, in which kids wore their hair short, respected the flag, were true to their school.

In the four years of the All-American Football Conference (1946–1949), the 49ers did not win a division, although they did advance to the 1949 championship game before losing to the Cleveland Browns.

Under coach Buck Shaw from 1946 to 1954, San Francisco was very competitive, with their best records being 12–2 in 1948 and 9–3 in 1949 and 1953. In the NFL, beginning in 1950, however, San Francisco was unable to reach the playoffs in their first seven seasons.

Frankie Albert, an All-American at Stanford and star quarterback for the 49ers from 1946 to 1952, was named head coach prior to the 1956 season. He led them to a disappointing 5–6–1 mark.

DID YOU KNOW...

That a little-known player from St. Mary's College named Al Endriss, who played briefly (1952) for the 49ers, became the greatest prep baseball coach in the history of Northern California? In 1976 Endriss, who also played in the Dodgers organization, was named National High School Coach of the Year, and in 1977 his Redwood Giants (Marin County) were named national champions by *Collegiate Baseball* magazine and the Easton Bat Co. In 1980 the *Sporting News* named Redwood the National High School Baseball Team of the Decade (1970s).

The Niners of the 1950s had an inordinate amount of talent. No less than six members of the team would go on to the Hall of Fame, and they were all career 49ers in their prime. What this says about the team, the coach, or their character is uncertain. In terms of superstars, Frankie Albert's team seems to match up well with Vince Lombardi's Packers, who dominated the next decade.

First there was defensive tackle Leo Nomellini, the first-ever 49ers draft choice when they joined the NFL. Actually born in the old country, he came to America with his family and to the 49ers out of Maryland. He played every single game for 14 seasons (1950–1963). Nomellini played 174 consecutive games and made 10 straight trips to the Pro Bowl before retiring at age 39. Nicknamed "the Lion," he was named to the All-NFL team on both offense and defense, and to the Hall of Fame in 1969.

Fullback Joe Perry was one of the groundbreaking black stars of the era. Born in Arkansas, he was part of the Westward migration of African Americans after the war, and came to the 49ers out of Compton Junior College in Southern California. From 1948 to 1960 Perry ran wild for the Niners. He was the first NFL player to rush for 1,000 yards in consecutive seasons. When he retired, his 9,723 career yards were second only to Jim Brown. Known as "the Jet," Perry entered Canton, Ohio, with Nomellini in 1969.

Halfback Hugh McElhenny was another of the stars produced out of the L.A. high schools, but he played collegiately at

The Lions' Yale Lary nearly intercepts a Y.A. Tittle pass intended for the 49ers' Clyde Conner during Detroit's 31–27 win at Kezar Stadium on December 22, 1957. This was San Francisco's first trip to the NFL playoffs— and they wouldn't return for another 13 seasons.

Washington before coming to San Francisco in 1952. He became one of the rare players to gain more than 11,000 career yards, and he scored 60 TDs, 38 on the ground. In his first preseason play he scored on a 42-yard jaunt. In 1952 McElhenny ran a punt back 94 yards and made an 89-yard run from scrimmage. He scored two touchdowns in the 1953 Pro Bowl after his rookie season.

Texas-born Y.A. Tittle came to San Francisco in 1951 from Baltimore, where he had signed out of Louisiana State. He played 17 years (10 with the 49ers), passing for 33,070 yards and 242 touchdowns.

110

Interestingly, while he is considered a 49ers legend and likely would have made it to Canton (1971) based strictly on his San Francisco years, his best seasons came after a trade to the New York Giants prior to the 1961 season. Coach Red Hickey decided to install the infamous shotgun. He traded the slower, pocket-passer Tittle in favor of young, athletic John Brodie, Bill Kilmer, and Bobby Waters. The shotgun was wildly successful before it was exposed as a failure. Tittle went on to earn NFL MVP honors that season. One of the most famous photos ever taken is a grainy, black-and-white, "last hurrah" depiction of a dazed, helmetless Tittle on his knees with blood on the side of his head after a hard hit in his final season.

Tackle Bob St. Clair was a native San Franciscan who played at USF and then the University of Tulsa. An offensive lineman, he also played goal-line defense. A hard-nosed type, he once lost five teeth blocking a punt without a face mask. He made All-NFL three times and the Pro Bowl five times.

Fullback John Henry Johnson was born in the South but came out West, where he played locally at St. Mary's before transferring to Arizona State. His first three years were with San Francisco (1954–1956). He was part of the famed "Million Dollar Backfield" of Tittle, Perry, McElhenny, and himself. Besides the 49ers, Johnson also toiled for Detroit, Pittsburgh, and Houston, scoring 48 career rushing touchdowns. In 1957 Johnson was a member of the Detroit Lions. In a season of inches, he was the margin of error between winning and losing.

Nineteen fifty-seven was a highly emotional year in which each game seemed to be a cliff-hanger. Tittle specialized in an alley-oop pass play to rookie halfback R.C. Owens. San Francisco split two games with archrival Los Angeles, winning at Kezar but losing before 102,368 at the L.A. Coliseum.

Beloved Tony Morabito died of a heart attack during the Chicago Bears game in October. Trailing 17–7, San Francisco

> **TRIVIA**
>
> What was the "all-initial backfield?"
>
> Find the answer on page 169.

fought back to win 21–17 with end Billy Wilson catching the winning pass in the fourth quarter.

On November 17 at Detroit the Lions handled them 31–10. The following week Johnny Unitas and Baltimore beat the Niners 27–21. The season appeared to be over in the face of a brutal four-game road trip, culminating in a challenging Thanksgiving weekend game with the New York Giants at Yankee Stadium.

The 49ers responded with a stirring 27–17 victory. Home wins over the Colts and Packers in front of capacity houses at the rickety Kezar Stadium lifted the club to 8–4 with a playoff berth at home against Detroit.

This was an opportunity to gain revenge for the 31–10 loss to the Lions, and when San Francisco jumped out to a 14–0 first-quarter lead, it looked good. Tittle completed 18 of 31 passes for 248 yards and three touchdowns. R.C. Owens caught a 34-yard touchdown pass. McElhenny and wide receiver Billy Wilson also caught scoring strikes. McElhenny had six receptions for 96 yards on the day. Gordy Soltau's 10-yard, third-quarter field goal seemed to have iced it at 27–7.

But just like the Roger Staubach comeback game of 1972, San Francisco refused to accept prosperity. Lions quarterback Bobby Layne led Detroit all the way back. Layne was cut from the old-school cloth—like Billy Kilmer (and later Ken Stabler)—a hard-charging partier with an eye for the ladies. He came out of the University of Texas, where he was an All-America quarterback and

WINNERS

Before there was Joe Montana—for that matter, before there was Willie Mays, Rick Barry, Reggie Jackson, Ken Stabler, Barry Bonds, or other great sports stars of the Bay Area—there was Frankie Albert. First, he quarterbacked Stanford under coach Clark Shaughnessy to their last national championship (1940). Following his All-America career, Albert served during World War II. After that, he was a star on the first 49ers team (1946), playing for them until 1952. He was their head coach from 1956 to 1958.

baseball star. Layne became a sensation in the NFL, a Hall of Famer. Perhaps his greatest moment came when he turned the wild cheers of 60,118 Kezar denizens into stony silence. Meanwhile, time after time the Detroit defense stiffened and held San Francisco.

Seemingly against all odds, Detroit mounted drive after drive. Two touchdowns came in the third quarter after Soltau's field goal, narrowing it to 27–21 entering the fourth period. By that time the momentum had swung. San Franciscans just sat there and watched it happen like a slow-motion car wreck. A touchdown and field goal iced it in the fourth quarter, 31–27. San Francisco would not see the playoffs for 13 more years.

SO CLOSE, AND YET SO FAR

Since the first Super Bowl was played at the Los Angeles Memorial Coliseum in January of 1967, no pro football team has ever won three straight. The Green Bay Packers won the first two, which when added to their 1965 NFL title still stands as the last of the "three-peat" pro football champions.

The 1971 through 1973 Miami Dolphins played in three straight Super Bowls, but lost the first one. Their bid for a third straight ended in the "Sea of Hands" loss to Oakland in the 1974 playoffs. Denver won two straight in recent years, but with John Elway's retirement they did not have what it took to maintain dominance.

In baseball, three-peats are relatively common. The A's did it from 1972 to 1974, the Yankees from 1998 to 2000; just to name two modern champions. The Boston Celtics and the L.A. Lakers have done it with relative ease in the NBA. Since the creation of the Associated Press poll in 1936, it has never happened in college football. The California Golden Bears (1920–1922) and Minnesota Golden Gophers (1934–1936) managed to win various forms of the national championship, but the 2005 Southern California Trojans missed their aptly named three-*Pete* by virtue of a nine-yard Vince Young touchdown run with 19 seconds left in the Rose Bowl.

In 1990 the San Francisco 49ers entered the season heavily favored to capture that elusive third consecutive Super Bowl.

Coach George Seifert was no longer a question mark, having directed his charges to the most impressive Super Bowl victory ever the previous season. At his disposal was less a football team and more of a display at the Hall of Fame museum in Canton, Ohio. These were not "over the hill" Hall of Famers. These guys were carving their statistics and accomplishments into their plaques week by week. Joe Montana was the league MVP, passing John Brodie's team record to reach 34,998 career passing yards. His 3,944 yards was a club single-season record. Jerry Rice was at the height of his considerable powers. Ronnie Lott did not miss a beat. Pro Bowl linebacker/defensive end Charles Haley had 58 tackles and an NFC-high 16 sacks. Linebacker Bill Romanowski had 79 tackles, while cornerback Darryl Pollard recorded 74 (72 solo). Running back Roger Craig set the team career receptions record, breaking Dwight Clark's old mark of 506. Guard Guy McIntyre was a Pro Bowl selection.

San Francisco started 10–0 and won all eight of their road games. They finished 14–2, the best record in the NFL for the second straight year. They captured their fifth straight Western Division title. The Rams were not even a rival anymore. It was their eighth division championship since Montana & Co. led the 1981 team to the Promised Land, and the 11th since the 1966 merger. In that period the Rams had won eight, Miami 13.

Before the season, there were some disruptions—holdouts, injuries, retirements, and of course the inevitable talk of "three-peat," a term that could not be marketed because Lakers basketball coach Pat Riley had trademarked the term, literally.

WINNERS

Roger Craig was a 6', 222-pound running back who came to the 49ers in the second round of the 1983 NFL Draft from Nebraska. He and Jerry Rice had great work ethics. Craig's chiseled body was almost a work of art and at one time graced many a bus stop and billboard when he did underwear advertisements in the City. He was All-Pro in 1985 and 1988. His last year with the 49ers was 1990.

Roger Craig looks for daylight during the 49ers' 15–13 loss to the Giants in the 1990 NFC Championship Game—a game that stopped San Francisco's quest for an unprecedented third straight Super Bowl title.

"There are always going to be disruptions," Seifert said. "Through the course of camp, and during the course of the season, we have to work with the players [who] are on hand and stay involved with our football. That's what we're here for.... These are all veteran players who have been a part of our program for some time. We look forward to them coming back and being part of this club again.... Just because they are involved in contract negotiations, and in some cases will miss some time in camp, I don't believe [that] will distract us from our ultimate goal.... We all have great expectations."

Offensive coordinator Mike Holmgren had his offense in place by 1990. The season opener was at New Orleans, and it looked like a Saints upset until San Francisco pulled it out with a late field goal, making it 13–12 before a stunned Superdome crowd of 68,629. A series of convincing and close wins followed, but throughout San Francisco always looked to be in control.

In November the Rams managed to win at Candlestick 28–17. A week later on *Monday Night Football*, a preview of things to come was held when Bill Parcells and his great defensive juggernaut, the Giants, came to town. San Francisco's 7–3 win made for a lot of nervousness. Here was one of, if not the finest offensive machines ever: Montana, Rice, Craig, Holmgren, 55–10 over Denver, and in front of their fans they were held to a mere touchdown!

A chance to match the 1984 record of 15–1 was lost in Game 15 when the Saints came marching in to San Francisco and took a 13–10 win. The 14–2 Niners dismissed Washington 28–10 in the first playoff game. As the team trotted off the field, the full-house home crowd chanted, "Three-peat! Three-peat!"

For the second time in less than two years, events beyond the world of sports interfered with a San Francisco sports team. In October 1989 the Loma Prieta earthquake had shook up a Candlestick Park crowd, then broken up a World Series won by the Oakland A's over the San Francisco Giants.

The week of the January 1991 NFC Championship Game, the United States began an air war in Iraq. But despite concerns over the war, the game had to be played. Again, it was the New York Giants. In 1986 their defense dominated while quarterback Phil Simms led them to a Super Bowl victory. This time, Simms was out with an injury, replaced by the serviceable Jeff Hostetler. The face of their team was linebacker Lawrence Taylor, a larger-than-life pro football star whose appetites off the field were matched only by his ability to dominate on the field.

It was a "War of the Worlds," as Dennis Pottenger called it in *Great Expectations: The San Francisco 49ers and the Quest for the "Three-Peat."* A battle between the East Coast and the West Coast,

NUMBERS DON'T LIE

14—49ers players selected All-Pro in 1990

between the philosophies of Parcells and—with all due respect to Seifert—Walsh, whose imprint was still all over the 1990 Niners.

It marked another New York–San Francisco grudge match, and would offer all the thrills of the classic 1962 World Series, won in seven games by the Yankees over the Giants.

There was another element of past-meeting-the-present, in that the Raiders lost to the Buffalo Bills in the AFC title game, played before the NFC match. In 1971 the Raiders lost to Baltimore in the AFC Championship Game the same day the 49ers lost to Dallas. In 1984 the 49ers lost to Washington in the morning, but the Raiders earned a Super Bowl berth in the afternoon. The 1991 Raiders loss to Buffalo eliminated the intrigue of an L.A.–San Francisco Super Bowl. A Giants victory meant an all–New York state game.

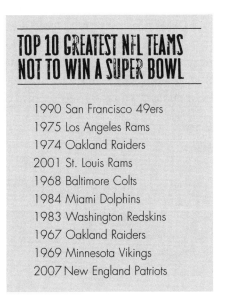

TOP 10 GREATEST NFL TEAMS NOT TO WIN A SUPER BOWL

1990 San Francisco 49ers
1975 Los Angeles Rams
1974 Oakland Raiders
2001 St. Louis Rams
1968 Baltimore Colts
1984 Miami Dolphins
1983 Washington Redskins
1967 Oakland Raiders
1969 Minnesota Vikings
2007 New England Patriots

San Francisco started the title bout with a drive resulting in a Mike Cofer field goal. New York lost their shot at a touchdown through self-inflicted wounds, settling for a field goal to end the first quarter at 3–3.

In the second quarter Hostetler hit tight end Mark Bavaro on key strikes, and Matt Bahr's field goal gave the Giants a 6–3 lead. Montana then led the 49ers on a late drive to send the teams into halftime tied 6–6. In the third quarter Montana hit John Taylor for a long catch-and-run touchdown over Everson Walls, the same defender who failed to stop Dwight Clark from making the Catch in 1982. A Giants field goal made it 13–9.

In the fourth quarter, holding a lead with the ball, Montana fumbled amid a furious rush from Taylor and Leonard Marshall.

Montana was forced out of the game with an injury. Hostetler, who earlier looked to have been forced out by injury, returned looking chipper. Then Bill Romanowski came up limping and was out of the game.

The Giants managed another field goal to narrow the score to 13–12. With 5:47 left, Steve Young was in. Roger Craig fumbled, and Lawrence Taylor recovered it at the New York 43 with 2:26 left to play. The Giants drove into field-goal range and broke 49ers hearts with a Matt Bahr kick to end the dreams of a third straight title, 15–13. They went on to beat Buffalo on a wide-right Bills field-goal try to take their second Super Bowl in five years.

IT AIN'T OVER 'TIL IT'S OVER

COMEBACK

Under coach Bill Walsh, the San Francisco 49ers won the Super Bowl in the 1981 and 1984 seasons. After both of those years, they experienced letdowns. In 1982 the NFL players struck, limiting the regular season to nine games. The Niners never got on track and failed to contend.

The 1984 team is considered by some to be the best ever. Unlike 1981, they were a perfect combination of youthful veterans, superstars, and team players; running and passing; quick-strike offense and stifling defense; and brilliant coaching. They were a dynasty, all but unbeatable. The great Dan Marino and his high-powered Miami Dolphins fell like the North Korean defenders at Inchon, with the MacArthur-like Montana leading San Francisco to resounding victory.

It seemed after that game nobody could stop San Francisco except San Francisco and their own hubris. In reality, the Niners did not completely fall apart in 1985 or 1986. The '85 Chicago Bears and '86 New York Giants were juggernauts who could beat anybody, which they did in those seasons.

By 1987, however, the 49ers appeared to be just another good team in a conference that had finally found its power base after years of falling to the AFC. Pundits questioned whether Walsh was looking for another challenge. Hotshot quarterback Steve Young was brought in by trade from Tampa Bay, causing immediate controversy. Having "failed" to lead his team to Super Bowl victories over the previous two seasons, Montana now faced the fickle San Francisco "What have you done for me lately?" crowd. Another strike hit in 1987, and again it seemed to throw the team off stride. The fractured season produced a Washington-Denver Super Bowl. John Elway, anointed as the next great quarterback—a "replacement" for Montana—was totally outplayed by Washington's Doug Williams, the first black quarterback to lead his team to a world title.

San Francisco's regular-season performance in 1988 had nobody talking about their place in history. The Niners opened 5–2 but slumped to 6–5, two games out of first place in the NFC West. Then they beat defending champion Washington to launch a four-game winning streak. Their 10–6 mark was good enough to capture the division crown, but they were not a big favorite to go all the way. That said, they had Montana and Rice. No one was betting against them, either.

San Francisco had the good fortune of getting healthy in time for the playoffs. Eric Wright had a combination of ailments and age plaguing him, but he was ready to contribute at the end. Tim McKyer was able to come into his own that year. John Taylor missed some games early but was back. Montana had a bad back, but Steve Young filled in nicely. Joe was ready to go for the playoffs.

The team was "very loyal to Joe," said Wright, an All-Pro cornerback. "We had played with him [Montana] over the years and in two winning Super Bowls, so we were supporting him 100 percent.

"We knew that when he was in there, we could be down by a touchdown with two minutes left, and he would bring us back."

The Rams had faltered late in the season to give San Francisco the edge they needed in winning the division crown, and with it home-field advantage rather than the wild-card. Neither Minnesota (34–9 loss at Candlestick) nor Chicago (28–3 losers) were a match for them.

The Bears game was a very important one in that it was played in freezing conditions at Soldier Field. Pacific Coast teams are

The 49ers celebrate the 10-yard Joe Montana–to–John Taylor touchdown pass that gave San Francisco a come-from-behind victory over the Bengals in Super Bowl XXIII.

notorious for their inability to meet the cold-weather challenge (see: Chargers, Rams), but the great ones do (see: 49ers, Raiders). With two weeks to rest and prepare, the Super Bowl now represented the prospect of a reward in the form of Miami temperatures.

However, the Miami experience was not all bikini-clad models and South Beach revelry. Race riots in Miami's Overtown section cast a pall over the proceedings, although the hotel of their opponents (Cincinnati again) was closer to the riots than was the 49ers'.

According to Wright, the team managed to enjoy the nightlife, but they maintained their work ethic through veteran

TRADING PLACES

In the 1981 draft, San Francisco got Chicago's second-round draft pick via trade. With it, they selected 6'1", 180-pound cornerback Eric Wright from Missouri. Dwight Hicks, Keena Turner, Carlton Williamson, and even Jeff Fuller may have been more heralded players in the 1980s than Wright, who was platooned depending on defensive play situations. "Football is not like other sports," said Randy Cross. "A baseball player can hit anywhere. A football player is part of a system." In San Francisco Wright's success can be attributed to his role in that system, which he thrived in from 1981 to 1990 (making All-Pro in 1985).

leadership, not heavy curfews. Bill Walsh was never big on that kind of thing, preferring to treat his charges like adults.

The Bengals featured a terrific southpaw quarterback, league MVP Boomer Esiason, and running back Ickey Woods. Cincinnati coach Sam Wyche had once been mentored by Bill Walsh when he was an assistant under the legendary Bengals taskmaster Paul Brown. What no one realized before the game was that it was Walsh's last as a pro coach, not to mention star center Randy Cross' final contest.

Cincinnati was not going to let Walsh's scripted offensive scheme roll out to a 20–0 lead out of the gate this time. Bad omens reared their ugly heads for the Niners when offensive tackle Steve Wallace broke his leg early. Then nose tackle Tim Krumrie broke *his* leg. The field conditions were not good as a result of a poor "vacuum system" put in place before the game. A lesser team would have been put off their game by the conditions and injuries. This team had Montana and Lott.

They "had to put it into your mind that was just a normal thing that happened in the course of the football game," recalled Wright. "We didn't want to be wary about the field because it would slow us· down."

The "trademark" opening drive for a TD did not happen, setting the team off its confident pace. Instead of allowing it to be "disconcerting," according to Wright, it was "just up to the defense to stop the Bengals' offense. Our defense prided itself on keeping the other team in check until the offense got going—that was a formula for winning."

Cincinnati got the ball, bound and determined to score and give their ebullient star, Woods, a chance to do the famed "Ickey Shuffle." He picked up yardage but was held short of the end zone.

Michael Carter, Charles Haley, Keena Turner, and of course both Wright and Lott came to play. Despite the ballyhoo of both teams' offenses, it was quickly determined that Super Bowl XXIII would be a hard-hitting, grind-it-out defensive battle. Because of the West Coast offense, featuring a short passing scheme and creative patterns, the 49ers were thought of as a "finesse" team, which of course is ridiculous considering the true nature of pro football. "But the defense wasn't like that," said Turner.

Lott was a maniac on the field. Corner Don Griffin and safety Jeff Fuller emulated him as best they could. Mike Walter and Turner would alternate, depending on whether it was a passing or running down. Jim Fahnhorst stayed in most plays.

The strategy was to play the fast Bengals receivers—Cris Collinsworth, Tim McGee, and Eddie Brown—aggressively instead of trying to contain them. It was risky but it worked. Collinsworth broke for a long gain early against Wright, forcing Eric to respect his speed.

Montana broke the early logjam by driving his team from inside their own 5 to a Mike Cofer field goal and a 3–0 lead. In the first half, Walsh stayed with ball

NUMBERS DON'T LIE

Most Super Bowl Championships
6—Pittsburgh Steelers
5—San Francisco 49ers
5—Dallas Cowboys
3—Oakland/Los Angeles Raiders
3—New England Patriots
3—Green Bay Packers
3—New York Giants
3—Washington Redskins

control: short passes and handoffs to Roger Craig (1,000-plus yards rushing that season) and Tom Rathman. San Francisco had a chance to create some breathing room, but Cofer missed an easy field goal. Then, after a long John Taylor return of a punt, they drove deep into Cincinnati territory only to lose a fumble. Jim Breech managed a field goal to tie it for Cincy 3–3 at the half. The announcers all expressed amazement that their prognostications of a wide-open offensive "bonanza," as Niners broadcaster Joe Starkey liked to call it, had not been realized.

Cincinnati established themselves as a major challenge, taking over in the third quarter. They maintained a nine-minute possession resulting in another Breech field goal to forge ahead 6–3. While the Bengals were disappointed not to have scored a touchdown, they had put Montana & Co. on their heels, forced to watch from the sideline, while wearing out the defense. The 49ers were listless and punted, but Bill Romanowski's interception of an Esiason pass reversed momentum at a critical juncture. Cofer's subsequent field goal tied it 6–6. It was obvious that this was shaping up to be a Super Bowl for the ages. Very few Super Bowls up to this point had lived up to the hype.

The hype was increased, and the Niners' momentum totally stifled when Cincinnati's Stanford Jennings ran the kick back all the way to make it 13–6. Luck then played a role. Montana veered away from the close-to-the-vest style he had heretofore employed, hitting Jerry Rice and Roger Craig with long passes to push close to the Bengals' goal. Then a Montana pass intended for Rice or Taylor was dropped by cornerback Lewis Billups. Given reprieve, Montana hit Rice for a touchdown to tie it 13–13.

Cofer missed a field goal, and Breech made his to give the Bengals a 16–13 lead, but most of the world had one thing on their minds as San Francisco took over with less than three and a half minutes remaining. Joe Montana, starting at his own 8-yard line, was in his element.

49ERS GREATEST OVERTIME GAMES

1980: 49ers 38, Saints 35
1990: 49ers 20, Bengals 17
1996: 49ers 19, Redskins 16

Montana, a legend, an athlete of mythological proportions, a San Francisco icon perhaps over and above all others—Walsh, Lott, Joe DiMaggio, Willie Mays, Barry Bonds—will be remembered for directing his team to four Super Bowl championships, countless big victories, and many "two-minutes drives." In 1982 against Dallas the Catch was thrown by him but pulled down by Dwight Clark. In the 1985 Super Bowl the Niners dominated from start to finish. Montana was less "clutch" in 1989 than he was polishing his Canton statue.

His performance down the stretch against Cincinnati in Super Bowl XXIII, however, epitomized his cool nature. One particular incident stands out above all others. He hit five passes in a row, several to Rice, and had his team driving. The mindset of the club had gone from that of a tying field goal to a winning touchdown. With time called on the field, Montana stood amid his "band of brothers," each looking at him as if he were Henry V at Agincourt.

Then Montana noticed the comic actor John Candy, at that time one of the biggest stars in Hollywood, standing on the sideline. "Hey, check it out," he remarked. "Isn't that John Candy?" With the weight of the world on his shoulders, Montana appeared to be as calm as a stargazer on Hollywood Boulevard. It was the roly-poly Candy, observing Montana, who realized he was in the presence of *true* greatness.

Having taken their "Candy break," San Francisco resumed the drive with cool efficiency. A long pass to Rice, almost a touchdown, put the ball inside the Cincinnati 20. Montana had done it to Sam Wyche's team in a similar manner in 1987. Everybody *knew* he would come through again. Montana hit Craig down to their 10. Now they had the field-goal option, but wanted a TD first and foremost. Timeout was called with less than a minute remaining.

Cincy figured it was Rice who had gotten all the throws in the drive. John Taylor went into the middle, breaking for a split second, which was all Montana needed to hit him in the end zone, breaking Bengals hearts.

Rice was named MVP, having caught more than 200 yards' worth of passes. Montana threw for more than 350 on the game, with two scores. Many 49ers say it was their sweetest victory of all, for good reason. They had struggled, yet succeeded. Walsh's retirement made him a rare thing in sports. Few leave on their own terms at the height of their success. Walsh had his detractors. He was a man of big ego and rubbed some the wrong way. His moniker, "the Genius," was felt to be over the top by some. It was not. He is to football what Steven Spielberg is to filmmaking, Ernest Hemingway to writing, Abraham Lincoln to statesmanship.

THE MELANCHOLY STORY OF JIM PLUNKETT

Jim Plunkett is not a 49ers hero. He is, in fact, a 49ers bust. There are no great stories of Jim Plunkett leading the 49ers to glory, or even much beyond marginal half-season success. But in a book called *The Good, the Bad, and the Ugly*, Plunkett cannot be fit into the *bad* or *ugly* categories.

Plunkett's story is a wonderful one, and while his 49ers history is not much to write home about, it is a part of the bigger, wonderful picture.

First, let it be stated that Jim Plunkett was born to be the 49ers' quarterback. He grew up in San Jose. While the 49ers are of course named after San Francisco, it can be argued that they belong more to the peninsula and the south bay than to the City proper. Candlestick Park is not officially in San Francisco. It is located on a patch of land that nobody ever really claimed; a previously uninhabitable piece of the bay actually. That's right, Candlestick is on a piece of "land" that did not always exist. It is *landfill*. The story about how this section of the bay became land is the story of political corruption and stupidity.

Developer Charlie Harney had a lot of dirt, but no place to put it. He was in cahoots with Mayor George Christopher. They decided they would dump Harney's dirt at Candlestick Point and build a stadium for the Giants on it. Owner Horace Stoneham was driven out there at 10:00 in the morning on a cloudless, calm day. Stoneham was sold on the idea. According to legend, Stoneham was "in his cups" by 4:00 PM, at which time Candlestick Point was fog-enshrouded in a driving windstorm, but the deal was done.

NUMBERS DON'T LIE

18.0—Gene Washington's 49ers record for average yards gained per catch in his career (1969–1977). In 1968 Washington hooked up with Stanford sophomore Jim Plunkett to lead Stanford to a 20–0 beating of California in the Big Game.

So where is Candlestick Park? Well, it is either unincorporated or part of a "town" called Brisbane, which does not seem to have much of anything other than a zip code. Of course, San Francisco International Airport is not in San Francisco, either. Like Candlestick, its location is confusing. Some say Burlingame, some say it's on unincorporated San Mateo County land. Of course, South San Francisco is not in San Francisco—but the City would never claim this blue-collar cultural nonentity, anyway.

The point is that the 49ers are kings in San Mateo County, Santa Clara, San Jose, Marin County...but not so much in San Francisco. Its fan base, its season-ticket holders, come more from the suburbs. San Franciscans from San Francisco are as likely to head north to the wine country on beautiful Indian summer game days as they are to make their way to Candlestick Park, which is easily accessible from the peninsula.

San Jose is 49ers country, an area known as the south bay, which spans roughly from Stanford University and southward. Plunkett starred at James Lick High School, but he was not the marquee quarterback in the Bay Area. That was Mike Holmgren, out of Lincoln High in San Francisco. Lincoln High, located near Golden Gate Park and Kezar Stadium, where the 49ers played until 1970, also produced coach George Seifert. Holmgren went for USC, but never won the starting job. He was a Trojan for four years, while fellow San Franciscan O.J. Simpson won the Heisman and his team the national championship. Holmgren later became a coach under Seifert, then led Green Bay to the 1996 world championship.

When USC went for Holmgren, Plunkett decided to stay in Northern California. Notre Dame showed interest, but there was little enthusiasm. They had all their eggs in Joe Theismann's basket.

"I rejected California because the free speech movement was underway in Berkeley, and I didn't want to be bothered by student protests.... I knew all along it would be Stanford," said Plunkett.

Stanford and the 49ers are almost joined at the hip. Frankie Albert, who led Stanford to football glory, was a star 49ers quarterback and later their coach. John Brodie was a hero at Stanford before leading San Francisco to three straight division titles (1970, 1971, and 1972).

Bill Walsh returned Stanford to success before leading the 49ers to ultimate glory, then returned to lead Stanford back to success. The 49ers won their second of five Super Bowls at Stanford Stadium. They train at Santa Clara, just a short drive from Stanford. It is a comfortable, affluent community, and members of the team have long been an integral part of it.

Plunkett had to fight for everything he had at Stanford. A Mexican American from a poor neighborhood, the product of an unglamorous high school program, with parents suffering from physical maladies, Plunkett felt out of place with the rich kids and scholars who populate the Farm.

But he outworked his competition, becoming the starting quarterback as a 1968 sophomore. He returned the Indians (they became the Cardinals in 1972 and the Cardinal in 1982) to national prominence. In 1970 he entered the season considered a Heisman hopeful. Plunkett was asked what was more important to him, the Heisman or the Rose Bowl. The Rose Bowl seemed a longshot, real estate seemingly endowed to the mighty University of Southern California, who had gone there so consistently under coach John McKay that the place was their second home field.

"The question had hardly left the writer's mouth when Jim replied, 'The Rose Bowl, because I can do that with my team,'" recalled Indians coach John Ralston. "That tells you something about Jim Plunkett. Tears came to my eyes."

Nineteen-seventy came to be known as the "Year of the Quarterback." Aside from Plunkett, the collegiate landscape was dotted with star signal-callers Archie Manning of Mississippi, Rex Kern of Ohio State, Lynn Dickey of Kansas State, Bill Montgomery

Jim Plunkett gets roughed up by Steelers linebacker Robin Cole during a September 1977 49ers loss to Pittsburgh. Plunkett had a short, disappointing tenure in San Francisco but found stardom across the Bay while leading Oakland to a Super Bowl title.

of Arkansas, Dan Pastorini of Santa Clara, Ken Anderson of Augustana, and of course Joe Theismann of Notre Dame.

But it was a dream year for Plunkett. First, he defeated the mighty Trojans to get Stanford into the Rose Bowl. Then USC beat Theismann and Notre Dame, which gave Plunkett the Heisman.

In the history of the Rose Bowl up until this time, there may never have been a bigger underdog than Stanford was against Ohio State. Woody Hayes' team was unbeaten and untied. His 1968 Buckeyes had finished No. 1 with sophomores. Now they were seniors, led by Kern and safety Jack Tatum, but Plunkett led Stanford to the stunning upset, ending their surefire national championship aspirations, not to mention infuriating Woody. He despised most everything on the West Coast, especially Stanford (by now home of much antiwar protest).

Despite all the talent at the quarterback position, it was Plunkett who was the No. 1 pick in the 1971 NFL Draft by the New England Patriots.

"Thus far, I believe, Jim Plunkett is the best college quarterback I have ever seen," said TV analyst Bud Wilkinson.

"Plunkett is the best pro quarterback prospect I've ever seen," said UCLA coach Tommy Prothro.

Plunkett played professionally for one decade prior to leading the 1980 Oakland Raiders to a Super Bowl title. In that decade, he had one legitimate highlight. That occurred in his very first game, the initial contest ever played in the brand new Foxboro Stadium.

The Patriots were one of the lowliest teams in pro football. Their opponent, arguably the most successful: the Raiders. Plunkett stunned the Silver and Black with a 20–6 victory in 1971. That was it, however. New England was an also-ran in the Plunkett years. He lost his job to Steve Grogan, who got them into the playoffs.

IF ONLY...

Niners coach Monte Clark, who directed the team to a respectable 8–6 record in 1976, had not been let go in a dispute with the ownership group, partly out of differences regarding the future of Jim Plunkett, he may have been the 49ers' coach for a number of years. If so, when the window of opportunity for Bill Walsh to take over had come, they might not have gone for the Genius, with results that surely would never have approached their 1980s success.

In 1976 Plunkett was traded to San Francisco in a widely heralded deal. He was still young. There was still enough luster, especially in the Bay Area, from his Stanford days to believe that the return home would mark his personal comeback and a return to contention for a franchise that had not been in the hunt over a three-year stretch.

The popular mythology is that Plunkett was a big-time bust in San Francisco, but before that happened, he returned hope to its fans.

Under new coach Monte Clark, Plunkett engineered a fantastic 6–1 start. The media was agog. All of his Stanford promise seemed to be coming to fruition in San Francisco. With the Raiders off to a fantastic start, talk of an all-California Super Bowl—to be played in Pasadena's Rose Bowl, the site of Plunkett's greatest triumph—had football fans giddy with excitement.

Then San Francisco fell flat with four straight losses. Plunkett was barely mediocre after that. The final 8–6 record was respectable, but not playoff-worthy. In 1977 Plunkett was a virtual non-factor. San Francisco lost its first five games, finished 5–9, and Plunkett was gone.

He was signed by Oakland, but became a Raider only after seriously thinking of retirement.

"I'd never been a Raiders fan," he explained. "Growing up, the 49ers were always my team. I didn't like that Raiders silver-and-black color scheme or the team's attitude."

For two years, his presence on the Raiders' roster was for all practical purposes nonexistent. Then in 1980 Ken Stabler was dealt to Houston, and Dan Pastorini, one of those Year of the Quarterback names from 1970, where he starred at Santa Clara, was brought in. Pastorini was at first inconsistent, then gone when he broke his leg. Oakland turned to Plunkett out of shear desperation.

In one of the greatest comeback stories ever told, Plunkett took charge and led the Raiders to the world championship. In 1983 he again took the L.A. Raiders all the way, beating another 1970 college quarterback, Joe Theismann, in the Super Bowl. He engineered winning Raiders clubs in 1984 and 1985, retiring an

TRADING PLACES

Jim Plunkett was acquired from New England for quarterback Tom Owen (1974–1975), two 1976 No. 1 draft choices, and 1977 No. 1 and No. 2 picks.

all-time Raiders great, a color analyst on their radio broadcasts, and an icon of the organization on par with Ken Stabler and Fred Biletnikoff.

Plunkett has remained a faithful Stanford alum, too. His 49ers past is downplayed. Neither the team nor Plunkett make much of it. He filled a dismal period between John Brodie and Joe Montana. Obviously, as his Raiders record proved, he could have, under the right circumstances, led San Francisco to success. In retrospect, a lack of supporting talent or great coaching was at least as much or more to blame for the failures of 1976 and 1977 as Plunkett.

He never did team with O.J. Simpson, who was brought on in 1978. The idea of a Plunkett-O.J. "dream ticket" might have seemed a nice idea, but the truth is the 1978 49ers could only be cured by something like, oh, a new coach named Bill Walsh and a new quarterback named Joe Montana...but what were the chances of such a thing?

RIVALRIES

THE NORTH VS. THE SOUTH

On December 10, 1949, the National Football League announced a merger with the young All-American Football Conference. With that, the Baltimore Colts, the Cleveland Browns, and the San Francisco 49ers went from the old AAFC to join the established NFL.

The 49ers were, in essence, the first "big league" team in the Bay Area. The San Francisco Seals, along with other teams in the Pacific Coast League, had long dominated minor league baseball, but MLB's Giants had not yet made their migration westward from New York. In football, California and Stanford—located in nearby Berkeley and Palo Alto, respectively—had at one time or another been powerhouses in the college ranks, but the NFL had not previously entered the Bay Area market.

In joining the NFL, the 49ers became only the second franchise located west of Chicago. The first was the Los Angeles Rams, which had relocated to California from Cleveland starting with the 1946 season. Remarkably, Cleveland had won its first NFL championship in 1945, but the team's owner, Dan Reeves, nonetheless thought that L.A. offered a more prosperous future for his franchise. The Rams found their greener pastures at the Los Angeles Memorial Coliseum, where they were an immediate Hollywood hit.

While the Niners could lay claim to being the first big-time professional team in the Bay Area, they quickly found themselves taking a back seat to the Rams in the world of California professional sports. It was part of a larger picture that would develop.

San Francisco had originally been *the* West Coast city. Gold was discovered not in Southern California but in Northern California. Sacramento was chosen as the state capital. San Francisco, some 90 miles to the west, was established as a major seaport, a center of trade and commerce. Los Angeles was a sleepy Spanish pueblo, it's desert population kept small because of a lack of fresh water.

The Transcontinental Railroad connected the East Coast and the Midwest not with Los Angeles but with San Francisco. It was built over the rugged Rocky and Sierra Mountain ranges. It could have been built through Texas, Arizona, Nevada, and the Southern California deserts, which would have been easier from an engineering standpoint. It was not, though, because the major political backer of the railroads was Illinois senator Abraham Lincoln. Senator Lincoln opposed slavery, and was determined that the biggest achievement of the young country would not be accomplished on the backs of slaves, who surely would have done much of the work, at least in the southern states.

After the Civil War, the demographics of San Francisco and Los Angeles began to take shape. San Francisco was the destination of northerners from Boston and New York who had supported the Union. Los Angeles took on a more Confederate flavor.

The University of California was built as a land-grant public university in Berkeley. In nearby Palo Alto, Leland Stanford, one of the major railroad men of the era, created a private university. Natural rivalries in sports emanated between California and Stanford.

FIGHTING MAD

Jack Reynolds got the nickname "Hacksaw" when, after a tough loss at the University of Tennessee, he took a hacksaw to his Volkswagen, cutting it in half.

SOMETHING TO SAVOR

Cornerback Bruce Taylor was the 1970 NFL Rookie of the Year.

The population was too small to justify a major public university in Los Angeles, but the Methodist Church, in cooperation with other religious denominations, did found the University of Southern California, a private school, in 1880.

Everything changed in the early 1900s. L.A.'s "city fathers" decided they wanted to be a major metropolitan center. In order to do that, they needed water. City engineer William Mulholland arranged for an aqueduct to divert water from the Owens Valley to Los Angeles. As the country mobilized by train, by automobile, by airplane, and through two world wars, the population kept expanding. The basin was boundless, allowing for growth to outlying areas. The Bay Area, on the other hand, was naturally enclosed by mountain ranges with a body of water in the middle of everything.

USC wanted to compete in football with Cal and Stanford. Prior to World War I, they periodically played those schools, but were not considered big time. The best football in the country in the years prior to and during World War I shifted not to Los Angeles, but to the Pacific Northwest, where the University of Washington had a 63-game unbeaten streak.

World War I had a major impact on Southern California. In 1919 UCLA was founded as the southern branch of the University of California. USC bid to become a major football power. They joined the Pacific Coast Conference. The L.A. Memorial Coliseum, as well as the Rose Bowl in Pasadena, were erected.

In the early 1920s California built their Memorial Stadium, and Stanford Stadium was constructed. Stanford tried to get the Rose Bowl shifted from Pasadena to its new stadium, but Pasadena's successful completion of the Rose Bowl stadium kept the game in the Southland.

The Cal teams of the early 1920s were the greatest college football teams ever seen up to that time, and to this day one of

The Rams-49ers rivalry was forged in the 1950s, when the teams were the only NFL franchises west of Chicago. This gang-tackle of L.A. running back Jon Arnett was a rare 49ers highlight during a 56–7 rout by the Rams in November 1958.

the best dynasties in history. The "Wonder Teams" captured three straight national championships (from 1920 to 1922), largely on the strength of the first "recruits," who had been "shipped" by train from Los Angeles and San Diego. It was the first time a college had actively found players from outside the area and persuaded them to come to their school to play ball. Until then, teams were fielded on the strength of whoever showed up for tryouts. Stanford under coach Pop Warner captured the 1926 national championship and bid for supremacy with their Berkeley rivals.

USC was unable to beat Cal and fared little better with Stanford, thus ensuring the firing of "Gloomy Gus" Henderson because he could not defeat the Golden Bears. They tried to hire Knute Rockne away from Notre Dame but had to "settle" for his friendly rival, Howard Jones, and a yearly home-and-home arrangement with the Fighting Irish.

This had the effect of turning USC into a national powerhouse. Cal and Stanford became jealous of the Trojans' success, and the rivalries became heated. In 1932 the Olympics came to Los Angeles, establishing L.A. as a sports capital that overshadowed San Francisco. Better Southern California weather helped create a larger population base, thus producing more great young athletes from the high schools. UCLA became a major power, as well.

Natural PCL rivalries existed between the Seals, Mission Reds, Oakland Oaks, Sacramento Solons, Los Angeles Angels, Hollywood Stars, and San Diego Padres. The rise of Hollywood gave the imprimatur of glamour and star power to Los Angeles, causing angst in San Francisco.

World War II led to population growth in the entire state but had a greater effect in the Southland. Politically, divisions were created. San Francisco's longshoremen's unions gave the area a more liberal bent. Los Angeles, long the destination of Midwesterners and Southerners, took on a more conservative identity. The Rose Bowl at first was a game that invited Southern teams, then Big Ten schools. Fans of those teams came, saw, and often stayed, reinforcing this demographic.

After World War II, California was recognized as an electoral juggernaut, leading to the rise of junior senator Richard Nixon, the vice president from 1953 to 1961 and president from 1969 to 1974. Conservatism took hold in the West. Arizona senator Barry Goldwater became the face of the movement.

In the 1960s political divides were further created in response to the Vietnam War and campus protests. This led to the election of Republican Ronald Reagan as California governor and then president.

Both Nixon and Reagan were products of the L.A./Orange County GOP base. Up until the 1980s, Northern Californians were frustrated by their lack of political power. Symbolically, this dynamic played itself out in sports, where L.A. teams tended to prevail at the pro and college levels, as well as in terms of Hollywood and business. In the 1990s a shift occurred, symbolized by the election of two San Francisco women, Dianne Feinstein and Barbara Boxer, to the U.S. Senate from California.

The first game ever played between the Los Angeles Rams and the San Francisco 49ers was on October 1, 1950, when 27,262 came out to Kezar Stadium (more or less a glorified high-school venue) and saw coach Buck Shaw's Niners beaten 35–14. At the glamorous L.A. Coliseum a little over a month later, the Rams prevailed again by a score of 28–21.

The first game ever played between the new Los Angeles Rams and the 49ers was on October 1, 1950, when 27,262 came out to Kezar and saw coach Buck Shaw's Niners beaten 35–14. At the Coliseum a little over a month later, L.A. prevailed again by a score of 28–21.

Movie glamour enveloped the Rams in the form of quarterback Bob Waterfield, a local hero from Van Nuys High School and UCLA. Waterfield was a fine signal-caller, but it was his girlfriend who had everybody going gaga. Jane Russell, the star of *Gentlemen Prefer Blondes*, was at the time one of the major sex symbols of a sex-obsessed era. Her star was made in maverick filmmaker/aviator Howard Hughes' film *The Outlaw*, which scandalized America by revealing Miss Russell in a low-cut blouse while the camera kept creeping closer.

Individual rivalries revolved around the question of: who was better, the Rams' Elroy "Crazy Legs" Hirsch or San Francisco's Hugh McElhenny? Things came to a head in 1957, the first playoff year in 49ers history. Coach Frankie Albert's 49ers defeated Los Angeles 23–20 in front of a sellout crowd of 59,637 at Kezar Stadium. On November 10, 102,368 packed the Coliseum to see the Rams extract revenge, 37–24. Sellouts at Kezar and crowds in the mid-90,000s marked the remaining years of the decade, with enormous attendance in the years since.

The Coliseum has reconfigured its capacity several times over the years. In the 1940s and '50s it held well over 100,000 fans, and topped the century mark in games between the Rams and 49ers, USC and Notre Dame, and the Trojans and Bruins. In the early 1960s the stadium was renovated slightly, making for a capacity that has at various times ranged from 92,000 to around 94,000.

In 1961 coach Red Hickey installed the shotgun, which was used effectively in dismantling Los Angeles to the delight of a Kezar sellout crowd of 59,004 by a 35–0 score. But two weeks later, Chicago defensive coach Clark Shaughnessy figured it out in a 31–0 whitewashing of San Francisco. It was a devastating setback, and the Rams got revenge before 63,766 in L.A. on November 12, winning 17–7.

This marked a reversal in fortunes. The Rams of the 1960s and 1970s earned the reputation of being the best organization in pro football. General manager Don Klosterman, under the ownership of Carroll Rosenbloom, created a business and on-field model that produced success. Led by coach George Allen, Los Angeles became the dominant West Coast team in the NFL. Attendance was always good. They made shrewd draft choices, good trades, and continued to retool year after year.

The 49ers floundered. Their stadium was a laughingstock. Still, all was not lost. Quarterback John Brodie was widely respected as one of the best in the game, as was All-Pro safety Jimmy Johnson. Despite having better teams, Los Angeles did not dominate San Francisco in head-to-head competition.

The Rams of this era featured the famed "Fearsome Foursome" of Roosevelt Grier, Merlin Olsen, Deacon Jones, and Lamar Lundy.

LEADERS

In 1969 the NFL's Most Valuable Player was Rams quarterback Roman Gabriel. John Brodie, despite leading the league in passing in 1965, was still a less-heralded signal-caller, but in 1970 Brodie was named the NFL's Player of the Year.

Then in 1969 the Rams twice knocked the 49ers off. Quarterback Roman Gabriel won the league MVP award. In 1970 San Francisco served notice that they would not be an also-ran any longer by defeating Los Angeles in convincing fashion 20–6 before 77,272 at the Coliseum.

However, when the teams met in San Francisco, L.A. returned the favor, 30–13. The Rams suffered a series of strange defeats under new coach Tommy Prothro, failing to win the Western Division of the new NFC, while San Francisco, at 10–3–1, earned its first trip to the postseason since the 1957 debacle with Detroit.

In 1971 and 1972 San Francisco won the division two more times playing at Candlestick Park, but were unable to beat the Rams. The Rams looked at times like a great team, but faltered too often, failing to capture a postseason berth in either of those years.

The next year San Francisco got very old very fast. John Brodie was on his last legs, while new Rams coach "Ground Chuck" Knox instituted a strong rushing attack with Lawrence McCutcheon, along with ball-control quarterback John Hadl, dominating regular-season play. Over the next years, Los Angeles extended their winning streak over San Francisco to 10 games (from 1970 through 1975).

The conundrum of the rivalry was symbolized by San Francisco's ending the streak with an improbable 24–23 win over the Rams in front of a throng of 74,064 Coliseum faithful. The 49ers were a dismal 5–9 team. The 1975 Rams are thought by some to be the best pro team *not* to win, or at least not play in, a Super Bowl. Led by superstar defensive end Fred Dryer, the

THE BEGINNING OF THE END

The December 11, 1989, *Monday Night Football* game at Anaheim Stadium, in which Joe Montana led San Francisco to an incredible 30–27 comeback win over the Rams, was in many ways the last straw, leading to the eventual, dismal loss of the team to St. Louis five years later.

TRADING PLACES

The Rams, after dominating the 49ers for years, must have been chagrined to see Charle "Tree" Young, Wendell Tyler, and Hacksaw Reynolds—all former Rams—become stalwart Niners on Super Bowl champions. It all happened on Georgia Frontiere's watch.

talented Hacksaw Reynolds, and Jack Youngblood, the '75 Rams were 12–2, having allowed the second-fewest points ever in a regular season up to that time.

The clubs split their 1976 wins in a season that saw Monte Clark's team go 8–6 with Jim Plunkett at quarterback. Pat Haden took over for James Harris in L.A. Haden had signed, along with USC teammate Anthony Davis, with the Southern California Sun of the now-defunct World Football League (who played their games in Anaheim). Now on the Coliseum turf where he led Troy to glory, he led the Rams to a division title, although their victory against San Francisco came in the Candlestick game. The Rams lost the NFC title game at Minnesota, a team that bedeviled L.A. in numerous postseason games of the era, often with weather favoring the Vikings, whether in Minnesota or California.

Over the next four years, as the Bill Walsh–Joe Montana transition took shape, San Francisco played Los Angeles competitively, but never beat them. Ray Malavasi took over the reins in Los Angeles, but the franchise changed drastically during this time.

The Rams brought in Joe Namath, the legendary quarterback who had led the New York Jets to a historic Super Bowl win over the Baltimore Colts in 1969. Hobbled by knee injuries, "Broadway Joe" was supposed to become "Hollywood Joe," but he did not "do business," to use a trade term.

The Rams won with their patented running game and great defense, trademarks of their team for years. From 1977 to 1979, they utilized different quarterbacks in the wake of the failed Namath experiment. In 1979 Vince Ferragamo, an L.A. kid from

FIGHTING MAD

Rams quarterback Jim Everett was supposed to lead the Rams to victory. Instead, despite great potential, the former Purdue star and his team continued to be patsies at the hands of the Steve Young–led 49ers. Talk-show host Jim Rome was merciless in his assessment of Everett, calling him "Chris Everett" in an emasculating reference to women's tennis player Chris Evert. In 1994 Everett had had enough, physically attacking Rome during an in-studio interview.

Banning High School (who briefly played at Cal) caught fire. The Rams beat San Francisco 27–24 and 26–20, en route to a "home" Super Bowl appearance against Pittsburgh at the Rose Bowl. Ferragamo was spectacular, but the combination of Terry Bradshaw–to–Lynn Swann was better.

In 1980 a huge shift in Southern California sports occurred when the Rams moved to Anaheim Stadium in the suburbs.

This left the Coliseum vacant, in a way. USC continued to play there, but UCLA moved to the Rose Bowl, leaving the Coliseum to 'SC and the Raiders, who moved to L.A. in 1982. Several games between the Raiders and 49ers at the Coliseum in the 1980s had strange overtones to them. Enormous crowds came out, but a gang element, centered on the Raiders "bad boy" image and silver-and-black color scheme, lent criminality to the proceedings. Watching the 49ers do battle in the Coliseum in games against a team other than the Rams was disconcerting, although they enjoyed their fair share of success.

But what was most disconcerting was the change in the Rams' ownership structure. In 1979 Carroll Rosenbloom, an expert swimmer, went for a dip in mild Florida waters and drowned. His wife, a former Las Vegas showgirl named Georgia Frontiere, assumed control of the team. The rightful owner of the Rams was Rosenbloom's son, Steve, but Frontiere manipulated the records and won a power struggle. Nobody has ever proved that she killed her husband for his money, but many throughout sports suspect just that.

"Georgia will meet her Maker," Rams star Fred Dryer said in 2000. "She will be judged for her actions."

Frontiere immediately pulled up roots, leaving the venerable Coliseum, trashing 30 years of Rams tradition, glory, and success, for the green pastures of Orange County. As if by divine intervention, the rivalry with San Francisco, which was barely even a rivalry when the team first moved to the Big A, switched gears. It become a rivalry again, then became something, like most everything the Walsh-Montana-Lott 49ers did in the 1980s, that was dominated by San Francisco.

The 1981 world-champion 49ers could point to several turning points. After losing the opener to Detroit and Game 3 to Atlanta, they found themselves beating Dallas handily and holding off Green Bay in Wisconsin, always a tough task. But their 20–17 win over the Rams marked the beginning of their wild ride, enthusing the Bay Area over their chances.

A home loss to Cleveland was followed by a 33–31 victory at Anaheim, and the team never looked back. As the 1980s developed, the 49ers-Raiders games began to take on more meaning. But by the decade's end, both the Raiders and Rams were in San Francisco's shadow.

The nail in the coffin came on January 14, 1990, at Candlestick Park. In a 14–2 campaign, one of their losses had come at the hands of Los Angeles, 13–12 in San Francisco. The Rams were led by coach John Robinson, who presided over a successful running game in Anaheim just as he had at USC.

The Rams advanced to the NFC title game, but were embarrassed by Montana and his mates, 30–3. San Francisco went on to more Super Bowl glory, then made a successful transition to Steve Young, winning another Super Bowl and more divisions in another winning decade.

The Rams dropped deeper and deeper into a hole. Frontiere was a laughingstock, which was the best thing people had to say about her ("gold-digging femme fatale" being a more serious handle). Hated by an entire region, she packed up the Rams' bags following the 1994 campaign and moved to St. Louis. At first, it looked like a desperate move. Her team was desultory, fan acceptance lukewarm;

the 49ers continued to dominate. Then in 1999 the world went topsy-turvy when her team won an improbable Super Bowl.

In the years since then, as the league has realigned divisions to match regions, the Rams-49ers rivalry sadly is, for the most part, a thing of the past. "Beat St. Louis!" does not resonate with San Franciscans the way "Beat L.A.!" does.

THE GREATNESS THAT IS, ER, WAS THE RAIDERS

The obvious, natural rival of the San Francisco 49ers always was the Los Angeles Rams. It was a fierce rivalry in the 1950s and early 1970s. In the 1960s the Rams were a dominant team, the 49ers an also-ran. When the 49ers tanked from 1973 to 1980, the rivalry more resembled class warfare, just as the Giants-Dodgers and Cal-USC rivalries too often involved politics, credit cards, and envy more than genuine on-field competition.

In the 1980s much of the edge was lost when the Rams went to Anaheim, where crowds sat on their hands and San Francisco established themselves as the football version of Patton's drive through the Rhineland. But when the Rams took off for St. Louis, it was over. Who cared anymore? It was a cryin' shame.

The 49ers have played many tough games, within their division, their conference, and in the postseason. But two teams aside from the Rams, and in fact with the Rams in St. Louis more so than ever, emerge in the historical memory as major rivals. Geography only plays a part in it. The San Diego Chargers and Seattle Seahawks occupy the same coast and time zone, but neither has ever emerged as a big 49ers rival.

Two teams have. The Raiders, partly because of their physical locale (the rivalry may have gotten more heated when they were in L.A.). The Cowboys, because of the fierceness of playoff games in the 1970s, 1980s, and 1990s.

The 49ers were none too happy when the Oakland franchise was awarded to the brand new American Football League in 1960. For 14 years San Francisco owned the growing market. When the AFL was announced, it looked at first like Minneapolis would get a team, but at the last moment they got an expansion NFL club, leaving Oakland available.

The Raiders certainly did not pose much of a threat at first. Somebody suggested that they be called the Oakland Señors, which begs the question as to whether there would ever have been such a thing as Señor Nation. At first, the Raiders—the name was a combination of somebody on the Oakland City Council having been a Texas Tech Red Raider alum, the seafaring nature of Jack London's old town, and the riff on "pirates"—played home games at Kezar to little fanfare.

Then they switched to a glorified high school field in Oakland named after an undertaker. But the 49ers were poor, and there was hunger for quality football. The East Bay long had no identity. "Lost Generation" writer Gertrude Stein stated "there is no there there." But that was before the Raiders came along.

When Al Davis took over as coach, then AFL commissioner, then Raiders managing general partner, all bets were off. He quickly turned the Raiders into a team that was vastly superior to the 49ers. They were exciting, the 49ers dull. Then Oakland built a modern stadium, the Oakland–Alameda County Coliseum. It was so much better than Kezar—or Candlestick, for that matter—as to be beyond dispute. Long before Joe Namath led the "Super Jets" to victory, the Raiders' superiority over San Francisco erased any real question that the American Football League was as good as the established NFL. It was.

Oakland had the Raiders, the Coliseum, then the A's. San Francisco had a bad Niners team, a bad stadium, and hippies urinating all over the park, which had no parking, by the way. Where was the comparison? There was none. They played each other in preseason games, and they were not normal exhibitions. Local pride was on the line.

Naturally, in the first year of the new AFC-NFC arrangement, in which there were interconference games between old AFL-NFL teams, the final game of the regular season was San Francisco at Oakland. It was an immediate barnburner.

To the delight of the league, the Raiders and 49ers both won their respective divisions. The great hope had been that the New York Jets and Giants would be natural rivals, but the Jets faltered. That rivalry has never met the intensity of the 49ers-Raiders feud.

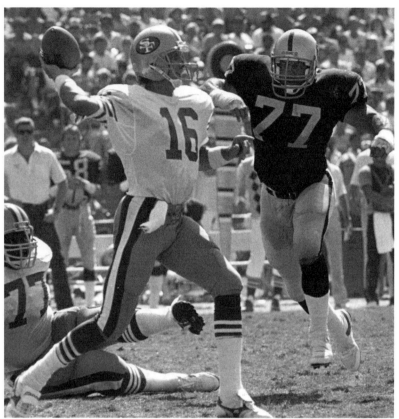

Lyle Alzado bears down on Joe Montana during San Francisco's 34–10 win over the Raiders in September 1985. The 49ers-Raiders rivalry reached its peak during the 1980s, when the two California franchises combined to win six of the decade's 10 Super Bowls.

There were fewer two-city—or even two-area—teams in pro football than there were in baseball. There were the Giants and Jets in New York and the Raiders and 49ers in the Bay Area. Chicago and Los Angeles had one team. Washington was close to Baltimore. San Diego sat by itself, never attracting much attention from L.A. even though the Chargers started out there. The Cowboys and Oilers played in the preseason and, in the 1970s it got rough when University of Texas Heisman winner Earl Campbell played for Houston, but it never took off much beyond that.

Social strata, envy, sophistication, blue collar versus wine drinkers, and of course the cold relationship that marked Lou Spadia and Al Davis gave the Raiders-49ers battles extra tension. In 1970 the crowd at the Coliseum was out for blood, but San Francisco needed a win to capture the division. They beat a Raiders team that had already clinched 38–7 in front of Oakland's loyal fans in a driving rain.

This created great hope that the two teams would meet in Super Bowl V. It was an open year, with no dominant teams. Both advanced past their first rounds but lost in their conference title games to end the dream.

Throughout the 1970s, the Raiders were a storied team, filled with legendary players, Hall of Famers. The 49ers floundered. The move to decrepit Candlestick was a slight improvement over Kezar (or was it?). But in the late 1970s Davis and NFL commissioner Pete Rozelle openly feuded over a legal issue called "eminent domain." The Los Angeles Coliseum was opening up with the Rams' rumored move to Orange County. The Raiders had a few down years, and the 49ers improved.

In 1980 the "greatness that is the Raiders," as Davis called it, was evident in their Super Bowl–winning performance. They seemingly rubbed it in the 49ers' faces by doing it with the recycled Jim Plunkett. In 1981, however, everything seemed to have swung San Francisco's way. Oakland had a down year. The 49ers were golden with Montana leading them all the way. When Davis announced his move to L.A. in 1982, it seemed like Rome outlasting Hannibal. The 49ers had won the long battle. In truth, the rivalry became hotter than ever.

Naturally, the first regular-season game ever played between Jim Plunkett and the brand new Los Angeles Raiders was against Joe Montana and the defending Super Bowl–champion San Francisco 49ers.

The Raiders, at least in those first years, fit L.A. like a glove. There was tremendous bitterness in Oakland, of course, but incredibly their fan base traveled, stayed loyal, and of course expanded in the Southland. All their games, home and road, were televised and broadcast on the radio, with longtime favorite Bill

King still calling the action. The uniforms were the same; the coach, owner, players, and personnel the same; even the stadium name—Coliseum—was the same.

In a hard-fought struggle, Los Angeles prevailed 23–17 at Candlestick. They put together an excellent season before getting upset by the Jets in front of more than 90,000 in a Coliseum playoff game. The 49ers stumbled badly at 3–6 in the strike-shortened season. In 1983, even though the two teams did not meet, it was as if Davis and the Raiders were telling San Francisco—along with Rozelle and all of pro football—"Hey, we're L.A., we're dominant, we're still the winningest team in pro football!"

What rubbed salt in the 49ers' wound even more was the fact that a team that had played in the cultural backwater of Oakland now played in the city that considered itself superior to San Francisco (San Franciscans schizophrenically switch back and forth from an inferiority to a superiority complex).

The 1983 Raiders captured their third Super Bowl title. Through the first half of the 1980s, the two best teams in football were the 49ers and Raiders. San Francisco rebounded to win the championship in 1984. The teams met again before 87,006 at the Coliseum in 1985 in a game that had all the earmarks of a rubber match.

Montana shut up the huge L.A. throng in a smashing 34–10 San Francisco victory, featuring all the tools of their Super Bowl greatness, not to mention a new receiver named Jerry Rice.

It would seem that was it, since San Francisco captured three more Super Bowls in the next decade while the Silver and Black have never recaptured the "greatness that is the Raiders."

In 1988, however, a year that saw the Raiders stumble and San Francisco capture the Brass Ring, Los Angeles won a defensive struggle at Candlestick 9–3. In 1994 the Super Bowl–champion 49ers embarrassed Los Angeles on *Monday Night Football* when Jerry Rice broke Jim Brown's all-time touchdown record in a 44–14 trouncing.

When the Raiders moved back to Oakland in 1995, they were trying to recapture lost magic. They never have. The preseason games and the occasional regular-season contests do not have the intensity of the old L.A.–San Francisco wars, but both teams, which have been down recently, will find their place in the sun again...maybe in a Super Bowl.

THE COMPUTER THAT WAS DALLAS

The 49ers' rivalry with the Dallas Cowboys has been a horse of an entirely different color from the one they have had with the Raiders. For one, the Raiders and Cowboys, aside from the fact that they are two of the winningest franchises in NFL history, are two teams with different images from top to bottom. Dallas is "America's Team," which is different from the "Raider Nation." The Cowboys, in theory at least, are squeaky clean, while the Raiders offer a criminal element...on the field and off. Of course, the Michael Irvin–led Cowboys of the 1990s were on as many police blotters as rosters. The Tom Landry teams were parodied as a façade, their coach a "Plastic Man" with a greater interest in computers than humanity. Several tell-all books and movies parodied Landry and the Cowboys. Then there are the cheerleaders. The Dallas Cowboys Cheerleaders are All-American girls. In Oakland, they could be found in *Playboy* or partying with the notorious Ken Stabler. In L.A., the Raiderettes were notorious for breaking the rules against fraternization with Raiders players.

CULTURE WARRIORS

The San Francisco–Dallas rivalry mirrored the larger California-Texas sentiments that have marked the two states, both of which entered the U.S. in the mid-19th century. In 1988 the Dallas Mavericks pushed the Los Angeles Lakers to seven games before losing in the Western Conference finals. In 2006 the Texas Longhorns knocked off the Southern California Trojans in a BCS Rose Bowl game that was probably the best college football game ever played. Texas is oil patch from the Gulf of Mexico to its northern borders. California outlawed most oil exploration after a spill off of Santa Barbara years ago. Party affiliation has switched. Texas used to be filled with LBJ Democrats, California with Reagan Republicans. Today Texas embodies "red state" Republican politics. California is reliably "blue state" Democratic.

The Cowboys are a team, like Notre Dame in college, that seems to have a rivalry with everybody. In the 1960s it was with the Green Bay Packers. In the early 1970s it was with the 49ers. In the mid-1970s it was with the Washington Redskins and the Pittsburgh Steelers. In the early 1980s and 1990s it was with the 49ers again.

The rivalry has always been infused by the cross-cultural differences of San Francisco and Dallas, California and Texas, "blue state" politics versus "red state" politics. Mayors and governors have gotten involved, betting cases of Napa Valley wine against boxes of USDA prime steak.

In 1970 the 49ers were an offensive powerhouse, led by quarterback John Brodie and receiver Gene Washington (both Stanford men). Dallas was a team in search of itself. In 1966 the Cowboys behind quarterback "Dandy Don" Meredith had advanced to the NFL title game, only to have Meredith's intercepted pass into the end zone with 28 seconds left deny them victory at the hands of the Packers.

Dallas was back in 1967, but this time it was the infamous "Ice Bowl" in Green Bay, the game where narrator John Facenda made his famous "frozen tundra" description. Cowboys wide receiver Bob Hayes was so cold he ran pass routes with his hands tucked into his shirt. Again, Dallas had victory swiped from them when Packers quarterback Bart Starr snuck over for a touchdown, 21–17.

The reason coach Tom Landry was given the moniker "Plastic Man" was because he rarely smiled, had little rapport with his players, and was one of the first coaches to rely on computerized information, for which he was lampooned. In truth, Coach Landry was a Christian who cared for his players but did not suffer fools well. Football coaches at every level eventually adopted his methods. His players found out he was a compassionate man who was there for them in later years when the money and the fame were not.

By 1970 he and the Cowboys were working on a reputation for not winning "the big one." That team was called the "Dallas Doomsday Defense." They recovered from a 38–0 *Monday Night Football* shellacking at the hands of the St. Louis Cardinals to finish 10–4, good for the division title. Quarterback Craig Morton,

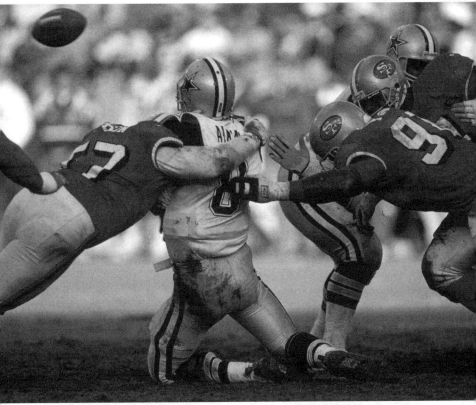

The San Francisco defense pummels Troy Aikman during the 49ers' 38–28 win over the Cowboys in the 1994 NFC Championship. The game propelled San Francisco to a Super Bowl win over the Chargers and was the only postseason blemish on what could have been a run of four straight NFL titles for Dallas.

an All-American at California, was a utilitarian pro. In the first playoff game, Dallas showed no offense, but allowed none either in a 5–0 win over Detroit. The 49ers surprised the 12–2 Minnesota Vikings on the road, returning to Kezar considered somewhere between even and the favorite to beat the Cowboys.

Dallas stuffed Brodie all day long. Morton was as good as he needed to be. Recalcitrant running back Duane Thomas, who represented a new kind of black athlete in the 1960s and 1970s, pointedly refusing to play for "the man," nevertheless ran wild for the ball-control Cowboys. The Niners scored a TD too late in a disappointing 17–10 loss. It was the final pro game at Kezar (although the high school "Turkey Day" game is still played there every Thanksgiving). The team and its fans would bid Golden Gate Park and the hippies adieu in favor of Candlestick the following year. The crowd, as if bound to live up to its rough reputation, was surly and drunk for the most part, chanting "Hurt Morton" as the game got away from the home team.

The Cowboys went to Miami, where they lost to Baltimore in what to this day is probably the sloppiest, worst-played Super Bowl ever played. They had every chance to win but blew it time and again, further adding to Landry's "can't win the big one" reputation.

In 1971 Dallas moved into Texas Stadium and replaced Morton with young hotshot Roger Staubach, who had done four years in the Navy before coming to the league. Staubach—disciplined, religious, and hard-working—was Landry's kind of guy. Meredith had been a hell-raiser. Morton was a party animal, too, although he later became as religious as Landry.

The 1971 Cowboys are considered one of the better teams in league history. It took them about seven games to find their groove and adjust to Staubach, who could throw, run, and think

HOME OF CHAMPIONS

After the Raiders won the Super Bowl in 1977, the Oakland–Alameda County Coliseum put up a sign that read "Oakland: Home of Champions," trumpeting the three World Series titles of the Oakland A's (1972, 1973, and 1974); the Golden State Warriors (who played in the next-door Coliseum Arena), winners of the 1975 NBA title; and the Raiders. Additional East Bay champs: California's football team won four national championships (1920, 1921, 1922, and 1937), its baseball team two (1947, 1957), its basketball team one (1959), and its track team one (1970, but taken away for NCAA violations). Until the 49ers won the 1982 Super Bowl, the west bay claimed only two University of San Francisco basketball titles (1955 and 1956), a couple of dusty Stanford national championships in football (1926 and 1940), one in basketball during the Paleolithic era (1942), and little else.

TRADING PLACES

Jim Plunkett led Oakland to the 1980 and 1983 world championships after failing in San Francisco. Ronnie Lott played for the Los Angeles Raiders after a stellar career in San Francisco. "Neon Deion" Sanders was a mercenary in San Francisco and Dallas. Ken Norton Jr. led San Francisco to the 1994 world championship after leading Dallas to the 1992 and 1993 titles. He later joined his '95 49ers defensive coordinator, Pete Carroll, on Carroll's staff at Southern California.

on the run, a rare combo, but when they hit all cylinders, there was no stopping them. The 11–3 Cowboys hosted the 9–5 Niners after both teams advanced past the first round. Dallas chewed San Francisco up and spit them out 14–3.

In 1972 the idea that a rivalry existed between the two teams seemed incongruous. The Cowboys ran their three-year playoff mark against San Francisco to 3–0, but the game was so wild as to reverberate through the ages. The 49ers led 28–13 entering the fourth quarter. Staubach, the Super Bowl MVP and future Hall of Famer, came off the bench and led Dallas to 17 points and a 30–28 win that ripped the hearts out of the 49ers. They never recovered, and would be a loser until the Joe Montana years.

That was when the rivalry resumed. Dallas achieved glory in the 1970s, although Super Bowl victories over Pittsburgh eluded them. The 1977 Cowboys, at 12–2, were a juggernaut that dismantled Denver, led by their old quarterback, Craig Morton, 27–10 in the Super Bowl.

By 1981 Staubach was retired, but Danny White offered a major challenge to San Francisco. In a see-saw battle for the ages, Montana led San Francisco downfield with the clock ticking away, hitting Dwight Clark with the Catch to clinch the 28–27 win. The roles were reversed. This time, the heart had been taken from Dallas, and they would not recover until the Troy Aikman era.

It was during this period that the rivalry hit its peak. Dallas fans were gaga over the return to glory of their beloved Cowboys, but victory in those days meant traveling a hard road through San Francisco. In 1992 and 1993 Dallas did just that. In so doing, Aikman established his Canton bona fides, Steve Young proved he was not yet at Montana's level, and Montana—sitting on the bench or playing in Kansas City—saw his legend grow in the City.

In 1994 Young's ascension to superstar status, despite years of glowing statistics and winning records, was not secured until Aikman and Dallas fell 38–28 at the 'Stick. Victory over San Diego in the Super Bowl was an afterthought.

In the years since, Dallas fell slowly but surely. San Francisco maintained a strong NFL presence, but Green Bay became the team to beat. Eventually, both teams became also-rans, with the rivalry spiced up not by legendary games for all the marbles, but by inane acts of unsportsmanlike conduct.

ODDS AND ENDS

THE SHOTGUN

George Halas and the Chicago Bears invented the T formation. With a few minor variations (consider John McKay and the I at USC), the T remains the standard offensive set to this day.

Before the T there was the "Yale wedge" (which was so dangerous that President Theodore Roosevelt proposed legislation to outlaw it), the "flying wedge," the "single wing," and others. The T formation created the modern quarterback—a signal-caller and offensive captain who generally took snaps from directly under center, then either handed it off to a running back (a halfback/tailback or fullback) or passed. If he ran, it was generally when flushed out of the "pocket," a "quarterback sneak," or possibly a called play that relied on surprise.

Over time, we have seen the veer, or wishbone, in which the quarterback is a running back charged with the split-second decision to run or lateral. The "run 'n' shoot" was popularized in the late 1980s and early 1990s but seems to have been solved. We also see a "shotgun" in which the quarterback stands a few yards behind center, taking a short snap, like a punter. The shotgun is generally viewed today as a late-game passing play, although some pass-friendly teams will run it throughout the game, sometimes in a no-huddle offense. A talented athlete like Vince Young when he was at Texas might orchestrate a run play out of it.

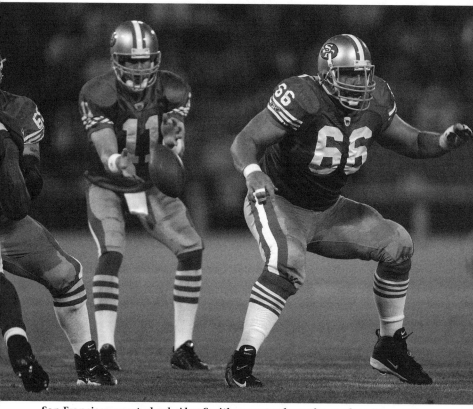

San Francisco quarterback Alex Smith operates from the modern incarnation of the shotgun formation during a September 2007 game against the Cardinals. The original shotgun, created by 49ers coach Red Hickey, was a sensation in 1960 and 1961—until opponents figured out how to defend it.

The original shotgun, however, was a wholly new concoction of San Francisco 49ers coach Red Hickey. It was wildly successful for a short time; was quickly figured out by the league; died an ignominious death; and in its original form has never returned at the pro, college, or to this author's knowledge, even high school level.

Hickey was creative, a top pass-receiver in his day. This broke the mold of old-time coaches in and of itself. A football coach was often viewed as a former linebacker or "defensive captain," calling signals in the manner of Tom Landry with the Giants. Or he might be a former quarterback. Receivers were considered too thin, too flaky, and too independent to make a good coach.

In the 1950s defense dominated the game. The famed New York Giants defense, the rising Packers of Vince Lombardi, and hard-nosed outfits in Baltimore and Detroit stunted the T formation. But Hickey saw a new game emerging, led by the large influx of faster players who were changing a power game into a speed game. This would be the impetus for success in the new American Football League, where the likes of San Diego's Sid Gillman, Oakland's Al Davis, and Kansas City's Hank Stram would alter the nature of offensive football forever.

But before there was Gillman, Davis, and Stram, there was Red Hickey. He surely had players who could run. One was J.D. Smith, and the other C.R. Roberts. At Southern California, Roberts had once rushed for 251 yards *in 12 minutes* in an antagonistic, racially charged atmosphere at Texas.

Hickey essentially came up with his revolutionary new idea out of desperation. In 1960 the Niners were going up against Johnny Unitas and the two-time NFL-champion Colts. San Francisco had made the playoffs three years prior, only to blow a seemingly insurmountable lead to Detroit. They were an also-ran, a second thought, laboring in West Coast obscurity. Midway through the week of the Baltimore game, Hickey came up with the shotgun.

When San Francisco knocked off Baltimore 30–22, the league took notice. He won four of the last five games of the 1960 season. He spent the off-season figuring out how to make the shotgun work more effectively, orchestrating his draft and roster around it.

First, he traded the venerable Y.A. Tittle to the New York Giants. He had a standard-issue drop-back quarterback out of Stanford, John Brodie, who was still athletic enough to run if he had to. Brodie was the quintessential Big Man on Campus— strong, good-looking, intelligent, with a "shotgun" for an arm.

Hickey drafted a wingback type from UCLA, Bill Kilmer. Kilmer could barely throw the ball; his passes looked like dying quails. He was not particularly fast, but he was the proverbial "eat nails for breakfast" guy who could play the game on guts, which, as the drill sergeant in *Full Metal Jacket* says, "is enough." Kilmer was a throwback, a beer drinker, a skirt-chaser at Westwood, a leader of the old-school variety.

Bobby Waters was a more natural tailback. Smith and Roberts operated as fullbacks at a time when that was still a running back position, not a blocking role. Five games into the 1961 campaign, the 49ers were 4–1. Rotating Brodie, Kilmer, and Waters on every play, while using Smith and Roberts in a combination of tailback plunges and wingback reverses, San Francisco led the NFL in points, passing, *and* running.

In the history of pro football, it could be argued that in that time frame they were the most unstoppable offensive juggernaut ever. The Detroit Lions and Los Angeles Rams, both strong clubs, fell in horrendous manner, 49–0 and 35–0, respectively. So overwhelming, so confusing, and so demoralizing was the 49ers' offense that it seemed to totally throw the *other team's offense* out of sync, as well. The league was in disarray. What to do about Red Hickey and the shotgun? There was talk about outlawing the darn thing.

Some coaches figured it was time to earn their paychecks, thus devising a way to take the bullets out of the shotgun. The theory of the formation is in three parts. First, receivers are draped all along the line where they can get downfield quickly. Second, the passer is back where he can survey the field from the start of the play. Third, the key maneuver rolls the passer to the side with a free choice to run or pass, similar to the "run 'n' shoot" later popularized by Mouse Davis and used in varying forms at Houston, Cal, Hawaii, and other college programs.

An option had been developed, forcing the defense to commit without blitzing, or hang back and give up ground. Also, linemen spread themselves out more in the shotgun offense. One end and the flanker are set wide. The two "running backs" are nearly on the line as wingbacks. The tailback is five yards back, alone. The play starts with a spiral snap to the tailback, who can step up to run or hand off on a wingback reverse, a real headache for defensive coordinators. Or he can halt and throw to a clearing field seemingly filled with receivers, wingbacks, and running backs coming out of the "backfield."

In the case of Smith and Roberts, their great speed created havoc. Hickey worked to keep the tailback "alive." He rotated Brodie, Kilmer, and Waters. On each play they were rested and

given marching orders from the sideline instead of picking themselves up, dazed after a hit, and heading back to the huddle to call
a play or accept one from a sideline emissary.

Brodie was best at passing. Kilmer was in those days a runner
(people who recall him when he was the quarterback of
Washington's Over the Hill Gang might find this hard to believe),
while Waters kept everybody honest.

Game 6 in 1961 was on October 22 against the Chicago Bears
at Wrigley Field. "Papa Bear" George Halas had by this time given
up the coaching duties and handed them to a man who was an
icon in the Bay Area. In 1940 Clark Shaughnessy had led the
Stanford Indians to the second of the only two national championships they have ever won. Knowing San Francisco was coming
up, Shaughnessy had been preparing since the off-season and
scouting it in detail for two weeks leading up to the game. He had
been "making a million diagrams," said Halas. "He threw out all
our old stuff and outguessed the 49ers."

Ironically, Shaughnessy is credited with "perfecting" the T
formation, which survived the shotgun like Britain withstanding
the Blitz.

"To pass the ball back to the tailback, the center has to put his
head between his legs, and nobody in that position can block a

HALL OF THE VERY GOOD

John Brodie was San Francisco's first pick of the November 27, 1956,
draft, coming to the 49ers fresh off the Stanford University campus. The
6′1″, 195-pound quarterback was a traditional drop-back passer. He
shared the so-called "quarterback" spot in Red Hickey's shotgun of
1960–1961, but in the aftermath of the loss to Chicago, Brodie became a
fixture for the team throughout the 1960s. A major talent, he was blamed
for his poor team's mediocre record, but when he had a cast to work with,
he led the 49ers to three straight division titles. In 1967 Florida's Heisman
Trophy winner, Steve Spurrier, showed up but was never able to wrestle the
starting spot away from the old veteran. Brodie was a star but has not yet
been accorded Hall of Fame status.

man that's on top of him," he said. "We put our middle line-backer, Bill George, right over the center. He was a great player with a quick sense of the game. More times than not, he just shot right through into the backfield. He had that poor tailback by the throat even before he could hand the ball off."

Shaughnessy also had his defensive linemen create a series of stunts, which he called "muddling," causing offsides penalties and confusion. The defensive ends spied on the wingbacks, with careful, planned substitutions quickly installed, depending upon the situation: Brodie in for a pass, a stiff front for Kilmer's runs, a balance for Waters.

The first quarter was scoreless, but Chicago forced a short punt, and a pass-interference call set up two touchdown passes by Bears quarterback Bill Wade.

"By the second half, they were discouraged," said Shaughnessy. "Our defense surprised them. As I always say, it doesn't make a heck of a lot of difference what you do, just make it new. Give them something they never faced before. They couldn't cope with it, and they just took it for granted that everything they did was wrong."

San Francisco's second-half offensive total: one yard. Their lone first down came via penalty. They lost several fumbles and interceptions. Chicago, constantly in good field position, cruised to a 31–0 rout.

The post mortems followed.

"It wasn't the 'defenses' that stopped our shotgun," said Hickey later. "We stopped ourselves. In that Bear game, we dropped the ball and threw it away. I abandoned the shotgun for three reasons. Bob Waters got injured, we were fumbling, and our confidence declined. Basically, the shotgun had worked because

CAN'T ANYBODY HERE PLAY THIS GAME?

In 1962 the 49ers were a dismal 1–6 at Kezar Stadium under coach Red Hickey. When Hickey's team lost the first three games of the 1963 season, he resigned and was replaced by Jack Christiansen.

HALL OF FAMERS

In 1973 Dave Wilcox posted 104 tackles, three for a loss, two interceptions, four forced fumbles, and one fumble recovery. His "final score," based on a grading system devised by the coaching staff, was 1,360. Prior to the season, it was felt the highest possible score was 750. Wilcox obviously earned All-Pro and a spot in the Pro Bowl. Considered one of the greatest outside linebackers of all time, in 2000 Wilcox was elected to the Hall of Fame. He played 11 seasons in San Francisco, earning seven Pro Bowl nominations and an equal number of All-Pro selections. In 1967 Wilcox won the Len Eshmont Award, named after a member of the original 1946 team. "Who was better?" than Wilcox, asked Dick Butkus. He was "one of the reasons I retired," said Mike Ditka. "I couldn't get off the line against him."

of confidence and aggressiveness. After a while, the kids read so much about the defenses catching up with the shotgun and solving it, they began to believe it. If the kids lost confidence in the shotgun, it was of no use to us. But I'll never keep losing with the same attack. Like I said after the Bear game, 'Next week we'll try something new. Blocking.'"

"I think it was a good formation," recalled Kilmer. "It had a lot of threats. The problem was they could key the quarterbacks. They knew Brodie would throw and I would run. I wish I could have run the option pass more."

Considering that Kilmer led Washington to the 1973 Super Bowl with a reasonable passing game (actually replacing the wunderkind Sonny Jurgensen), his idea may have had merit.

"Hickey never should have dropped the shotgun, just because we came along and surprised them," said Shaughnessy. "It's a sound formation with good values. He could have changed it enough to take advantage of the new defense. It's too bad."

In 1969, in anticipation of the 50-year anniversary of the National Football League, the NFL commissioned and prepared a coffee table–sized book on the history of the pro game. One of the chapters covered the shotgun and the 31–0 Bears win over the

49ers. It was written as "ancient history," but a few years later the shotgun reappeared, mainly in Dallas with runner-passer Roger the Dodger Staubach orchestrating it. Since then, many teams have adopted it either as their primary offensive set or as part of a variation. It has never been the juggernaut that it was for five games in 1961, but as Shaughnessy said, it had "good values" and with tinkering has never been stifled in the manner the Bears did that fall day in '61.

"MARSHALL'S RUNNING THE WRONG WAY!"

The San Francisco 49ers have benefited from some excellent radio announcers over the years. One of them was also the voice of Stanford; another the voice of Cal. Don Klein was an authoritative voice who called some of Stanford's greatest moments. He was on the scene in 1981, when Bill Walsh and Joe Montana led San Francisco to a magical season.

Joe Starkey is the longtime voice of Cal Bears football. In 1982 he called the phantasmagoric final touchdown of the Big Game between Cal and Stanford. It came to be known as "the Play."

"The band is on the field!" Starkey screamed as the last of myriad Cal lateralists scored on a kickoff to give the Golden Bears an improbable win in Cardinal quarterback John Elway's last college game.

But the greatest of all 49ers announcers, one of the greatest of all Bay Area broadcasters and in fact one of America's finest sports voices, was Lon Simmons. Simmons was and remains a class act of the first order. For countless members of the media, venturing into the cloistered world of the field, the dugout, the clubhouse, it was the 6'4" Simmons, the most respected and beloved of all media people, who welcomed them. He often introduced himself, instead of the other way around. He would present young writers and broadcasters to others, to players, making them feel welcome. He remembered names and made people feel like big shots with his hearty welcomes upon subsequent visits to the stadium. This is a business in which fellow writers and reporters are notorious for treating newcomers with suspicion and contempt. Simmons was well beyond such banality.

Lon Simmons ranks among the all-time greatest Bay Area sports broadcasters. The long-time voice of the 49ers, Simmons is probably better known for his work with baseball's Giants. Simmons is shown in 2004 after receiving the Ford C. Frick Award at the National Baseball Hall of Fame induction ceremony in Cooperstown, New York.

Simmons grew up in Fresno. He was a baseball pitcher recruited by Rod Dedeaux and USC. "Dedeaux came to see me," he recalled. "I pitched a game and threw about 155 pitches, struck out a lot of guys, walked an equal number. I think we won 9–8."

His pitching career never materialized, so he went into broadcasting. He became a reporter with KMPC, the flagship station of Gene Autry's Golden West Radio Network. Simmons was able to land a dream job—calling San Francisco Giants games in the broadcaster's booth with Russ Hodges and Bill King. In the history of sports radio, there may never have been three greater talents in the same booth at the same time.

Hodges and Simmons are Hall of Famers. If there is any justice, the late King will be. Hodges called Bobby Thomson's famed "Shot Heard 'Round the World" in 1951, famously exclaiming that, "The Giants win the pennant! The Giants win the pennant!"

King came out of the Midwest and Army radio service to the Bay Area in the 1950s. He announced Cal football when they went to the Rose Bowl in 1959 with quarterback Joe Kapp. Later that year he announced Cal's national championship basketball season under legendary coach Pete Newell. He became famous as the voice of the Oakland Raiders and Golden State Warriors. He did Oakland A's games for years before his untimely passing in 2005.

While King's tenure with the Giants was short-lived, Simmons became a staple. He and Hodges were like bees and honey—the mentor and his protégé. They called great Giants teams of the 1960s, the famed "bye, bye baby" era of Willie Mays, Willie McCovey, and Juan Marichal.

There came a time in which Simmons' dry humor was not well understood. The Giants of the 1970s were boring, and Lon sounded like it. Some thought he was drinking in the booth.

DID YOU KNOW...

That when this author pitched in a major league spring training exhibition game for the Oakland A's against the San Francisco Giants in 1981, my three innings of scoreless work were announced back to the Bay Area by no less than Bill King and Lon Simmons?

Eventually, as if to change his pace, Lon moved across the bay and spent some time in the 1980s announcing A's games. Oakland had competitive teams during this era. In subsequent years, Lon returned to the Giants, sometimes for extensive periods, other times as a guest announcer or a part-timer. Even when he moved from Alameda (his longtime home was in Half Moon Bay before that) to Hawaii in the 2000s, he felt the call, returning occasionally to do interviews and Giants games.

TAKE THIS GAME AND...

Mike Shumann, a member of the 1981 world champion 49ers, became a well-respected San Francisco TV sportscaster. Gary Plummer, a linebacker on the 1994 49ers world champions, became the team's radio color analyst.

Lon Simmons is best remembered as the voice of the Giants. Baseball was perfect for him, in that the languid, between-pitches nature of the game allowed him to tell stories, wry jokes, and observe the social scene. With age, maturity, and familiarity, his jokes went from being received with silence to knowing laughter.

But Simmons was an excellent football announcer, as well. He is famed in the annals of NFL Films for a call he made at Kezar Stadium in 1964. The 49ers were playing the Minnesota Vikings when the Vikings' Jim Marshall scooped up a fumble. Turned sideways and around by confusion, Marshall ran in the wrong direction.

"Marshall's running the wrong way!" he exclaimed, his voice cracking with excitement, a trademark of his that broke from the usual laconic style.

Simmons was the voice of 49ers football in the lean Kezar years, as well as the three consecutive division champions of the 1970, 1971, and 1972 seasons. Like King, his role was bigger than current announcers, because in those days home games were not televised, even if they were sold out.

He again presided over a doldrum period, from 1973 to 1980. In 1981 Simmons hung up his microphone and was replaced by Klein. Many felt that the 49ers Super Bowl victory was not complete without Simmons handling the broadcaster's duties, just as the 1976 Raiders had finally reached the Promised Land in a year in which stalwarts Jim Otto and George Blanda finally retired.

But Simmons, who could never retire or relax, was drawn back to the booth—to Oakland, to Candlestick, to Pac Bell Park—and in 1988 was there to tell the world about one of Walsh's most exciting teams, his last world champions.

CELEBRITY CORNER

It is appropriate that in a book titled *The Good, the Bad, and the Ugly*, in a section about celebrities who root for the San Francisco 49ers, the most identifiable San Francisco image is that of Clint Eastwood. His 1966 Sergio Leone "spaghetti Western" of the same name has become a touchstone cultural phrase that describes most everything in life.

Eastwood may be the most accomplished Hollywood figure of all time, surpassing the actor he is most often compared to, John "the Duke" Wayne. Eastwood has longevity, box-office success, critical praise, Oscars, and diverse achievement. He was the leading box office name in the 1960s, 1970s, and 1980s. He is one of the most successful directors in Hollywood history, and has done it all: screenwriting, producing, television work.

Eastwood is a Bay Area native who graduated from Oakland Tech High School, which produced A's superstar Rickey Henderson along with a number of other sports stars. Drafted into the army, Eastwood landed soft duty: lifeguard at the Ft. Ord swimming pool near Monterey. Honorably discharged, Eastwood—tall, ruggedly handsome, chiseled features, muscular with *perfect* hair—blew into Hollywood like so many other hopefuls.

He was discovered and immediately cast as a cowboy type: Rowdy Yates in *Rawhide*. By the mid-1960s he was a well-known, successful TV actor. He starred in a moderately successful film, *Coogan's Bluff*, playing a "duck out of water" cowboy investigating a crime in New York City. It became the template for the Dennis Weaver TV show, *McCloud*.

Then Eastwood had the opportunity to star in a series of Westerns made improbably in Spain. *The Good, the Bad, and the*

NUMBERS DON'T LIE

Completion percentage: Steve Young, 65.8 (1987–1999)
Yards: Joe Montana, 35,124 (1979–1992)
Touchdown passes: Joe Montana, 244 (1979–1992)

Ugly was the third and best of those. Directed by Leone, it was one of those movies that might be described as "so bad it was good."

To this day, the film is regularly shown on a big screen in San Francisco's Matrix, an upscale Triangle bar located where the old Pier Street Annex once was. On crowded Saturday nights, surrounded by young professionals and mingling singles, film buffs are often mesmerized by the "silent" film, mouthing the words of Eastwood and Eli Wallach.

TOP ALL-TIME 49ERS QUARTERBACK RATINGS

1. Steve Young, 101.4 (1987–1999)
2. Joe Montana, 93.5 (1979–1992)
3. John Brodie, 72.3 (1957–1973)

"Blondie, you can't die, Blondie," people will mimic Wallach when he tries to revive the thirsty Eastwood, who he previously left for dead in the desert, but must keep alive when he discovers that "Blondie" knows where the treasure is buried. Hilariously, groups of guys at Matrix will repeat the words while their irritated dates stare at them impatiently.

By the late 1960s, Eastwood's films were the leading money-makers in the world. Then in late 1971 came the movie that defined the actor, identifying him with the City. The screenplay was written by a USC film school graduate named John Milius, who attended USC with George Lucas.

Milius created "God's lonely man," who bucks the rules, the trends, and the coddling of bad guys. He set the film in San Francisco, using corrupt city officials, inept police brass, and odd bystanders as props for a tall, handsome, rugged macho man known as "Dirty Harry" Callahan. It was the role Clint Eastwood was born to play.

One of the most famous of all scenes from *Dirty Harry* is filmed right there on the 49ers' home turf, Kezar Stadium. Andy Robinson was given the role of "Scorpio," a take-off on the real-life serial killer who dubbed himself the "Zodiac Killer." Director Don Siegel chose Robinson because he wanted "a murderer who looks like a choir boy."

America fell in love with the movie and the actor. The love affair continues to this day. All the subsequent *Dirty Harry* films were shot in San Francisco or Northern California. Eastwood moved to the Monterey area, where he eventually was elected mayor of Carmel as a moderate Republican. His real-life politics never matched the ferocity of most of his characters.

Aside from Eastwood, many other celebrities have rooted for the 49ers. This includes local favorites like Chris Isaak, Huey Lewis, and all the band members of Journey, all of whom have sung many National Anthems.

TRIVIA ANSWERS

Page 24: Joe Montana had to beat out Tom Clements, Rusty Lisch, and Gary Forystek to become a starter at Notre Dame.

Page 84: Randy Cross was All-Pro six times (1980, 1981, 1984, 1985, 1986, and 1988). He was a 6'3", 245-pound center who helped Dick Vermeil's UCLA Bruins win the 1976 Rose Bowl, after which he was drafted in the second round by San Francisco. A close friend of Joe Montana's, Cross was handsome and erudite, later taking his personality into the broadcaster's booth.

Page 111: The all-initial backfield included quarterback Y.A. Tittle and running backs R.C. Owens, C.R. Roberts, and J.D. Smith. The 49ers also featured the "Million Dollar Backfield" and the "Fabulous Foursome."

NOTES

THE GOOD

"I could never describe in words what it was like," Clark recalled. Tuckman, Michael W. and Jeff Schultz. *The San Francisco 49ers: Team of the Decade.* Rocklin, Calif.: Prima, 1989.

"That was a little depressing," said linebacker Keena Turner. Tuckman, Michael W. and Jeff Schultz. *The San Francisco 49ers: Team of the Decade.* Rocklin, Calif.: Prima, 1989.

"I kinda like when that happens," Montana said. Tuckman, Michael W. and Jeff Schultz. *The San Francisco 49ers: Team of the Decade.* Rocklin, Calif.: Prima, 1989.

"Hold it or throw it high" so that "it'll be thrown away" instead of intercepted, with another play to go to if this failed, according to Walsh. Tuckman, Michael W. and Jeff Schultz. *The San Francisco 49ers: Team of the Decade.* Rocklin, Calif.: Prima, 1989.

"I thought I had jumped too soon," recalled Clark, but he came down with it. Tuckman, Michael W. and Jeff Schultz. *The San Francisco 49ers: Team of the Decade.* Rocklin, Calif.: Prima, 1989.

"It was definitely a new experience for us," said Keena Turner. Tuckman, Michael W. and Jeff Schultz. *The San Francisco 49ers: Team of the Decade.* Rocklin, Calif.: Prima, 1989.

"We felt satisfied that we'd done what we wanted to do in the first half," recalled Fred Dean. Tuckman, Michael W. and Jeff

Schultz. *The San Francisco 49ers: Team of the Decade*. Rocklin, Calif.: Prima, 1989.

"From that point on, we realized we could win this thing," said wide receiver Mike Shumann. Tuckman, Michael W. and Jeff Schultz. *The San Francisco 49ers: Team of the Decade*. Rocklin, Calif.: Prima, 1989.

"My father wasn't always telling me to win, win, win—he wasn't force-feeding me," he said. Montana, Joe. *Audibles*. New York: William Morrow and Co., 1986.

Montana "may be the greatest player who ever the played the game," said broadcaster and former Bengals receiver Cris Collinsworth. Montana, Joe and Richard Weiner. *Art and Magic of Quarterbacking*. New York: Henry Holt, 1997.

"C'mon, are you kidding me?" Walsh asked in mock amazement when posed this question at 49ers headquarters in Santa Clara, California, in April of 2001. Travers, Steven. "Genius Bids Adieu." *San Francisco Examiner*, April 20, 2001.

"Al Davis is a fascinating man, a true football genius who I admire greatly," said Walsh. Travers, Steven. "Genius Bids Adieu." *San Francisco Examiner*, April 20, 2001.

"From all I've read about Bill's Cincinnati experience, it must have left a lasting impression on him," said Montana. Montana, Joe and Bob Raissman. *Audibles: My Life in Football*. New York: William Morrow, 1986.

"We 'beat people to the punch,'" said Walsh. Walsh, Bill and Glenn Dickey. *Building a Champion*. New York: St. Martin's Press, 1990.

"There was a Camelot quality to USC at that time," said his coach, John Robinson. *History of USC Football* DVD.

"There's no way I was going to take Kenny Easley over Ronnie Lott!" Walsh exclaimed years later. "Are you kidding me?" Travers, Steven. "Genius Bids Adieu." *San Francisco Examiner*, April 20, 2001.

"Engaged in action during a game I'm lucky, in a sense, because my body will help me deal with pain." Lott, Ronnie and Jill Lieber. *Total Impact*. New York: Doubleday, 1991

"That loss catapulted us to the next year, our championship

year," recalled quarterback Steve Young. Peary, Danny ed. *Super Bowl: The Game of Their Lives*. New York: Macmillan, 1997.

THE BAD

The friendship between the two men, and Sayers' impassioned love of Piccolo, was embodied by his memorial words, "I am third," a reference to Piccolo and God coming ahead of him. www.galesayers40.com

Thus was "T.O." born. Black Book Partners, LLC, 2004.

"Football's religion in the South," said Jackson. Travers, Steven. *September 1970: One Night, Two Teams, and the Game That Changed a Nation*. Lanham, Md.: Taylor Trade Publishing, 2007.

THE UGLY

He often hung out around Candlestick, frequently enough to befriend the great Willie Mays, who followed his high school and junior college careers with interest and declared, "You have an unusual talent." Travers, Steven. *The USC Trojans: College Football's All-Time Greatest Dynasty*. Lanham, Md: Taylor Trade Publishing, 2006.

SOMETHING TO SAVOR

Wide receiver Jerry Rice, by 1990 established not only as the finest wide receiver in the NFL but already eliciting commentary that he might be the greatest ever, was "almost inhuman to me," said Millen. Peary, Danny ed. *Super Bowl: The Game of Their Lives*. New York: Macmillan, 1997.

It was a team of leaders: Lott, Montana, Randy Cross, but "everybody on that team knew his job without anybody saying anything to them," said Montana. Peary, Danny ed. *Super Bowl: The Game of Their Lives*. New York: Macmillan, 1997.

"We had to guard against getting excited, although we knew we were the world champs," said Millen. Peary, Danny ed. *Super Bowl: The Game of Their Lives*. New York: Macmillan, 1997.

"Growing up in a small town taught me the meaning of doing the right things," he said. Rice, Jerry and Michael Silver. *Rice*. New York: St. Martin's Press, 1996.

"I can't think of another player that more exemplifies the drive, work habits and commitment it takes to reach the top," said former 49ers assistant Mike Holmgren. Rice, Jerry and Michael Silver. *Rice*. New York: St. Martin's Press, 1996.

Montana was nervous about Young, for obvious reasons, even though Walsh told the media, "We fully expect Joe to continue as the leader and mainstay of our team." Livsey, Laury. *The Steve Young Story*. Rocklin, Calif: Prima, 1996.

WHEN THE FAT LADY SINGS

"There are always going to be disruptions," Seifert said. Pottenger, Dennis. *Great Expectations*. Rocklin, Calif: Prima, 1991.

IT AIN'T OVER 'TIL IT'S OVER

The team was very "very loyal to Joe," said Wright, an All-Pro cornerback. Peary, Danny ed. *Super Bowl: The Game of Their Lives*. New York: Macmillan, 1997.

Instead of allowing it to be "disconcerting," according to Wright, it was "just up to the defense to stop the Bengals offense." Peary, Danny ed. *Super Bowl: The Game of Their Lives*. New York: Macmillan, 1997.

"Football is not like other sports," said Randy Cross. Tuckman, Michael W. and Jeff Schultz. *The San Francisco 49ers: Team of the Decade*. Rocklin, Calif: Prima, 1989.

"I rejected California because the free speech movement was underway in Berkeley and I didn't want to be bothered by student protests..." Plunkett, Jim and Dave Newhouse. *The Jim Plunkett Story*. New York: Arbor House, 1981.

ODDS AND ENDS

He had been "making a million diagrams," said Halas. *The First 50 Years: The Story of the National Football League*. New York: Simon & Schuster, 1969.

"It wasn't the 'defenses' that stopped our shotgun," said Hickey later. *The First 50 Years: The Story of the National Football League*. New York: Simon & Schuster, 1969.

"I think it was a good formation," recalled Kilmer. *The First 50 Years: The Story of the National Football League.* New York: Simon & Schuster, 1969.

"Who was better?" than Wilcox, asked Dick Butkus. *2000 San Francisco 49ers Media Guide.* San Francisco: San Francisco 49ers, 2000.

ABOUT THE AUTHOR

teven Travers, a former professional baseball player with the St. Louis Cardinals and the Oakland A's organizations, is the author of more than 15 books, including the best-selling *Barry Bonds: Baseball's Superman*, nominated for a Casey Award as Best Baseball Book of 2002; and *One Night, Two Teams: Alabama vs. USC and the Game That Changed a Nation* (a 2007 PNBA nominee, subject of the CBS/CSTV documentary *Tackling Segregation*, and soon to be a major motion picture). He has written numerous books for the Triumph/Random House *Essential* and *The Good, the Bad, and the Ugly* series. He pitched for the Redwood High School baseball team in Marin County, California, that won the national championship in his senior year, before attending college on an athletic scholarship and earning all-conference honors. A graduate of the University of Southern California, Steven coached at USC, Cal-Berkeley, and in Europe; served in the army; attended law school; and was a sports agent. He has written for the *Los Angeles Times* and was a columnist for *StreetZebra* magazine in L.A., and the *San Francisco Examiner*. His screenplays include *The Lost Battalion*, *21*, and *Wicked*. Travers is a guest lecturer at the Annenberg School for Communications at the University of Southern California. He has a daughter, Elizabeth Travers, and lives in Marin County, California.